# The Memry

Integrated Approach
to ISO 9001:2008
Quality Management Systems Standard

**James (Jim) W. Collins, Jr.**
Plexus International, Inc.

**Dolores Sherwood Steiger**
Plexus International, Inc.

First Edition Authors

Robert W. Peach, Robert Peach and Associates, Inc.

Bill Peach, QA International Ltd., Inc.

Diane S. Ritter, Ritter Resources

Second Edition | GOAL/QPC

**The Memory Jogger™ 9001:2008**

Development Team
Susan Griebel, *Project Leader*
Michele Kierstead, *Illustrator*
Janet MacCausland, *Illustrator | Designer*
nSight, Inc., *Project Editor*

GOAL/QPC
12 Manor Parkway, Salem, NH 03079-2841
Toll free: 800.643.4316 or 603.893.1944
Fax: 603.870.9122
E-mail: service@goalqpc.com
www.MemoryJogger.org

Printed in the United States of America

*This book was originally published as*
The Memory Jogger™ 9000/2000

Second Edition
10 9 8 7 6 5 4 3 2

ISBN: 978-1-57681-112-2

# ⚜ Acknowledgments

Our sincerest thanks to the people and organizations who have contributed their insights, suggestions, and encouragement or who gave us permission to use and adapt their tips, charts, tables, and other illustrative information.

*Concept & Content Reviewers*

Paul Amaral, *Texas Instruments, Inc.*; Captain Brian Basel, *U.S. Coast Guard Headquarters*; Michael Brassard, *Brassard & Ritter, LLC*; Frank Caplan, *Quality Sciences Consultants, Inc.*; Tom Condardo, *ZBR Publications, Inc.*; Robin Crusse, *U.S. Coast Guard*; Ross Gilbert, *GE Medical Systems*; George Haire, *Mine Safety Appliances Co.*; Dr. Craig Johnson; Linda Johnson, *Allegro MicroSystems, Inc.*; Kevin Lange, *General Physics Corp.*; Herbert Monnich; Johnny Morris, *Shep Enterprises*; Darwin Newell, *Dover Corp., Cook Division*; Paul O'Donnell, *U.S. Coast Guard*; Elizabeth Potts, *Ashland Chemical Co.*; Jan Pruett, *BellSouth Telecommunications, Inc.*; R. Daniel Reid, *General Motors Corporation*; Curtis Ricketts, *State of North Carolina Department of Labor*; Gary Roberts, *Apple Computer, Inc.*; John Stratton, *Eastman Kodak*; Joseph Tiratto, *Joseph Tiratto and Associates*; Joseph Tsiakals, *Amgen*; Steve Walsh, *Ford Motor Company*.

*Contributors*

Robert Belfit Jr., *Omni Tech International*; Jane Belmondo, *Belmondo & Associates*; Frank Caplan, *Quality Sciences Consultants, Inc.*; David Erdman, *MacDermid, Inc.*; *DaimlerChrysler*; *Ford Motor Company*; *General Motors Corporation*; Ross Gilbert, *GE Medical Systems*; William Howarth, *D.B. Riley, Inc.*; Linda Johnson, *Allegro MicroSystems, Inc.*; Ann Phillips,

Omni Tech International; Dolores Steiger, *Plexus International*; Sam Tolbert, *Scientific Atlanta*; William J. Vance, *Haworth, Inc.*; Steve Wirkus, *Advanced Cardiovascular Systems, Inc.*

**Second Edition Content Reviewers**
Margot Bumpus, PAE, *a Lockheed Martin Company*
Debbie Dean, FAA/*Academy*
Brian Hettrick, *Soma Associates*

**Publishers**
ASQ; CRC Press; Information Mapping; Irwin Professional Publishers; Marcel Dekker Publishers; McGraw-Hill.

## Editor's Note

Jim Collins of *Plexus International, Inc.*, has edited and updated this second edition of this Memory Jogger, originally titled *The Memory Jogger*™ 9000/2000, to bring the latest version of the ISO 9000 standards to light. The original authors Robert Peach, Bill Peach, and Diane Ritter, now in conjunction with Jim Collins, have combined their talents to produce a readable, user-friendly guide for all of those involved in the process of adopting and using ISO 9000. Robert Peach is an original member of the ISO committee that developed the ISO 9000 Quality Systems Standard, and editor of *The ISO 9000 Handbook*. Bill Peach is a consultant with QA International Ltd., Inc., and previously managed quality for FTD. Diane Ritter is a coauthor of *The Memory Jogger*™, *The Memory Jogger*™ II, *The Creativity Tools Memory Jogger*™, and *The Problem Solving Memory Jogger*™.

# ⟡ Authors' Note

From concept to publication, this book is the result of the collaborative effort of a "virtual" team. Phones, faxes, computers, postal mail, and e-mail all played a part in connecting the GOAL/QPC home office in New Hampshire to the writers in North Carolina, Michigan, Minnesota, Mississippi, and Georgia, and in connecting the writers to their many friends and colleagues scattered across the nation.

All this was possible because of the quality and standardization of the many systems and processes in place. For that, we are grateful to the concepts and tools of Total Quality Management and ISO 9000 standards.

To our friends and colleagues who have read the manuscript or provided material, we thank you for your knowledge, thoughtfulness, honesty, insight, and suggestions.

And for the continued love, support, and extreme patience they have shown throughout this project, we owe a special note of thanks to:

*Shirley Peach & Mary Ann Lee*
*Paul, Christian, Karin & Lauren Ritter,*
*and Jacqueline Denise Collins*

We are forever in your debt.

*Robert W. Peach*

*William S. Pesch*

*Diane S. Ritter*

*James D. Ralph*

The Memory Jogger™ 9001:2008 | ©2009 GOAL/QPC

# Table of Contents

Acknowledgments ........................................ iii

Editor's and Authors' Note .......................iv

How to Use
  The Memory Jogger™ 9001:2008 ......... viii

*Part One*...........................................................1

1. Introduction ......................................... 1

2. The Process Approach............................15

3. Auditing and Registration....................71

*Part Two* ........................................................93

4. Quality Management System ............95

5. Management Responsibility .............109

6. Resource Management .....................123

7. Product Realization ..........................131

8. Measurement, Analysis
   and Improvement ...........................187

9. ISO 9001:2008 Continual
   Improvement Efforts ........................225

10. Additional Resources .....................241

*Refer to the chapter opening pages for detailed contents*

## How to Use
# The Memory Jogger™ 9001:2008

The Memory Jogger™ 9001:2008 is a convenient and quick reference guide to use on the job. It is intended to serve as a reminder of the things you have already learned through training, reading, or experience.

➤➤ If you are interested in a specific topic, refer to the chapter title pages for a detailed list of the contents. The corner of each chapter title page is blue.

## Who Should Use This Book?

Much has been written to describe how to make use of the ISO 9001 Quality Management Systems Standard. Almost all of those resources were written for *the few people* in an organization who are responsible for guiding the implementation effort; however, in the end, *every member of the company will be affected.*

Unlike other resources, *The Memory Jogger*™ 9001:2008 was written for a broad audience, including managers, implementation teams, supervisors, staff, and all others who need to understand what **they** must do to actively contribute to the implementation and registration effort of ISO 9001.

### A Note to ISO/TS 16949 Users

*The Memory Jogger*™ ISO 9001: 2008 would be useful to ISO/TS 16949 users because the Technical Specification includes all of ISO 9001, verbatim. The additional requirements of the Technical Specification are supplemental to, and more prescriptive than, the requirements of ISO 9001. ISO 9001 provides descriptive requirements for a Quality Management System (QMS), whereas ISO/TS 16949 requirements are more detailed and tailored by, and for, the automotive industry. For more information, see *The Memory Jogger*™ TS 16949:2002 at **MemoryJogger.org**.

# Chapter
## ONE

# INTRODUCTION

What does ISO mean? ............................... 2
What is ISO 9000? ................................... 2
What is a Quality Management System? ........ 3
What are the ISO 9000 Core Standards? ......... 4
Relationship of QMS to Environmental
Management Systems .............................. 5
Why adopt ISO 9001:2008? ....................... 7
Certification versus Registration ................. 8
Quality Management Principles ................... 9
Lessons Learned ..................................... 14

Customers and global competition are changing the way organizations around the world are doing business. Quality is leading that change—providing quality products and services to keep your customers coming back. However, quality doesn't happen just because you talk about it.

To achieve quality, you must work at it by understanding your processes—the work you do every day—and continually improving them.

Standardizing your work into an organized and documented system can provide the foundation for a comprehensive quality management program. The ISO 9001 *Quality Management Systems* (QMS)—*Requirements* are helping organizations do just that!

## What does ISO Mean?

ISO is recognized as the short name for the International Organization for Standardization, an international agency within 160 member bodies. ISO derives from the same Greek root as the prefix to the words *iso*bar, *iso*metric, and *iso*sceles, which mean equal pressure, equal measurements, and equal sides to a triangle; that is, things that are equal. The United States' representative to ISO is the American National Standards Institute (ANSI). ISO works to promote the development of standards, testing, and certification to encourage the trade of conforming products and services: state to state and country to country around the globe.

## What is ISO 9000?

The core of the ISO 9000 Quality Management Systems Standard consists of five international standards that provide guidance in the development and implementation of an effective and efficient QMS. Not specific to any particular product or service, these standards are applicable to manufacturing and service industries alike.

# ⟶ What is a Quality Management System (QMS)?

QMS refers to the activities you carry out within your organization to satisfy the requirements and expectations of your customers. To ensure that you have a QMS in place, customers or regulatory agencies may insist that your organization demonstrate that your QMS conforms to the ISO 9001 model.

Complying with the ISO 9001 standard doesn't indicate that every product or service meets the customers' requirements, only that the QMS in use is capable of meeting them. Your organization must continuously assess how satisfied they are and demonstrate constant improvement measured against their feedback.

Evidence of your compliance with the ISO 9001 standard is first gathered by your internal auditors. This is called "first-party auditing" and is part of the requirement of the Standard. It requires you to select, train, evaluate, approve, and continually reevaluate your internal auditors. At times, a customer will check your compliance to the Standard. This is referred to as "second-party auditing." You may choose to do second-party auditing of your own suppliers. When a registrar body sends an auditor(s) to confirm your compliance to the Standard, this is called "third-party auditing." When a registrar finds that your organization fulfills the requirements of the ISO 9001:2008 Standard, your organization becomes "registered" and receives a certificate that should satisfy your customers who require evidence of ISO 9001 compliance. Companies not concerned with becoming registered may, nevertheless, want to comply with ISO 9001 as a continual improvement business model.

## What are the ISO 9000 Core Standards?

- **ISO 9000:2005** provides QMS principles and fundamentals, describes what the series is about, and lists basic definitions of terms for use by any organization.

- **ISO 9001:2008** states QMS requirements which explain when an organization must demonstrate that it is capable of effectively and efficiently meeting customer, statutory, and regulatory requirements.

- **ISO 9004:2000** provides guidance for establishing a QMS that goes beyond ISO 9001 requirements by improving the efficiency of the system. ISO 9004 is being revised as of the printing of ISO 9001:2008 and the release of this edition of *The Memory Jogger*™ *9001:2008.*

- **ISO 10012:2003** provides controls and guidance for the measurement system in its publication, *Measurement Management Systems—Requirements for Measurement Processes and Measuring Equipment.*

- **ISO 19011:2002** provides guidance on planning and conducting audits of quality and/or environmental management systems.

## QMS Requirements

Whereas ISO 9001:2008 is a requirements standard, ISO 9000, ISO 9004, ISO 10012, and ISO 19011 are guideline standards. ISO 9001 specifies the requirements for a QMS, not how to set it up.

ISO 9001:2008 includes five primary sections that contain 23 sub-clauses (see chapters 4 through 8). These requirements define what your organization must do to conform to the Standard. Many of these requirements must be documented and controlled.

# Relationship of QMS to Environmental Management Systems

Environmental Management Systems (EMS) identify, collect, and integrate an organization's individual environmental programs so that the overall operation of those programs is effective and efficient.

An organization may have in place a number of independent compliance programs, such as:

> Waste water discharge
>
> Hazardous material handling
>
> Solid waste disposal
>
> Airborne emissions

Once the EMS is in place, the organization has a foundation upon which to expand other environmental programs, such as:

> Recycling
>
> Pollution prevention

Energy conservation

Environmental awareness

Many of these expansion programs are of the type that can encourage large economic returns.

A family of environmental management standards has been developed by ISO Technical Committee 207 on environmental management. By intention, the paragraph structure of the Standards upon which these environmental management systems are based has been harmonized with that of QMS, so that an organization may administer EMS and QMS programs as parallel activities, should it choose to do so.

Harmonization includes auditor training criteria, as well as course provider and registrar accreditation processes. The United States has established an organizational liaison to the quality and environmental working groups developing and administering management systems standards to minimize duplication of effort. A list of the ISO/TC 207 standards issued as of this printing is on page 240.

As with ISO 9001, environmental management standards do not dictate the actual performance standards to be met, such as for air and water quality, but they coordinate processes and procedures to verify that systems exist for meeting national environmental performance standards.

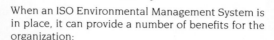

When an ISO Environmental Management System is in place, it can provide a number of benefits for the organization:

- A process for identifying and managing its significant environmental aspects

- A system for meeting key environmental policies, objectives, and targets

- Emphasis on prevention rather than correction

- A system for producing evidence that reasonable care and regulatory compliance exist

- A system for continual improvement of the EMS and environmental performance

It is possible to combine your QMS and your EMS into one system. See ISO 19011 for guidance on how to audit a combined QMS and EMS.

## Why Adopt ISO 9001:2008?

Organizations adopt ISO 9000 standards for different reasons. Your organization's decision to do so may be to:

- Comply with customers who require ISO 9001

- Compete in domestic and worldwide markets

- Improve your business management system

- Minimize repetitive auditing by similar and different customers

- Improve suppliers' performance

- Improve organizational performance

Both you and your organization benefit because use of ISO 9001:2008 serves as a basis to:

- ❖ Understand and communicate what processes you use to produce products or provide services
- ❖ Achieve better understanding of and consistency across all QMS practices
- ❖ Ensure continued use of the registered QMS on a yearly basis
- ❖ Improve the effectiveness of documentation
- ❖ Improve quality deployment
- ❖ Strengthen organization/customer confidence and relationships
- ❖ Yield cost savings and improve profitability
- ❖ Form a foundation and discipline for improvement activities within the QMS

Of course, these benefits are achieved only with good planning, aggressive implementation, hard work, and continual improvement.

## Certification versus Registration

For some users of ISO 9001:2008, the term certification is synonymous with registration. The certification of your QMS does not certify your products or your employees; instead, it confirms that your business management system meets the requirements of ISO 9001:2008.

To avoid confusion, many organizations choose to use the word *registration* for the process of meeting the requirements of the Standard.

# Quality Management Principles

The following eight principles have been identified by the ISO quality standards technical committee to facilitate achievement of objectives.

ISO 9001 contains a large number of requirements and methods aimed at improving quality management capabilities. But the number of principles is small. Methods may change or evolve, but principles do not. Users of ISO 9001:2008 should familiarize themselves with each principle, assuring that methods put into use are consistent with these QMS principles.

## ■ *Principle A—Customer Focus*

### *What this means:*

↠ Understand the needs of current and future customers

↠ Meet all customer requirements

↠ Strive to exceed customer expectations

### How do I do it?

↠ Recognize that survival is based on dependence upon the customer

↠ Achieve conformity

↠ Target customer perceptions

↠ Formally review contracts

↠ Record and analyze complaints and returns

↠ Offer consumer value through preferred products and services

## ■ Principle B—Leadership

### What this means:

- ➦ Establish unity of purpose and direction for your organization
- ➦ Set policy and objectives
- ➦ Establish your organization's internal culture, in which employees are partners in achieving the organization's objectives

 **How do I do it?**

- ➦ Set clear goals and objectives…have an organizational "compass"
- ➦ Treat quality as a strategic issue
- ➦ Provide human and physical resources in order for your organization to achieving its objectives

## ■ Principle C—Involvement of People

### What this means:

- ➦ Fully develop the abilities and competencies of our greatest asset—our people
- ➦ Give them the freedom to use their abilities to achieve maximum benefit

 **How do I do it?**

- ➦ Maintain a high level of communication between leadership and employees

- Ensure that process operations are understood by all

- Integrate your human resources plan with your strategic business plan

- Conduct active and value-added training and process qualification activities

- Encourage employees to contribute to your organization's improvement strategy

- Align employees' daily work tasks with the overall objectives of the organization

### Principle D—Process Approach

**What this means:**

- Manage resources as though they are processes

- Support processes that yield more effective and efficient results

 **How do I do it?**

- Carefully define and measure each process and all performance parameters

- Optimize the resources of each process

- Ensure that final products and services meet requirements

- Control each process itself, not just its output; correlate measures at key points in the process using process output measures

---

## ■ Principle E—System Approach to Management

### What this means:

- ↔ Identify, understand, and manage the interrelated processes of a system to effectively and efficiently attain objectives

 **How do I do it?**

- ↔ Recognize the need to coordinate/link key processes

- ↔ Verify that customer needs are being met

- ↔ Validate not only production processes, but also other processes, including design, development, and delivery

## ■ Principle F—Continual Improvement

### What this means:

- ↔ Make improvement a permanent objective for the organization

 **How do I do it?**

- ↔ Focus on process improvement to achieve business results

- ↔ Provide resources to ensure that targets are met

- ↔ Develop and operate mature corrective and preventive action loops

- Continue to improve the effectiveness and efficiency of the QMS

- Strive to achieve stretch improvement goals

- Seek to prevent defects, and to reduce variation and waste in the supply chain

### Principle G—Factual Approach to Decision Making

**What this means:**

- Base decisions on logical analysis of objective data and information

 **How do I do it?**

- Focus on data such as audit results, performance reviews, corrective actions, and complaints to improve customer satisfaction

- Observe short- and long-term trends and indicators of performance

- Use data to continually improve your organization's performance

### Principle H—Mutually Beneficial Supplier Relationships

**What this means:**

- Create value through mutual, beneficial, interdependent relationships with suppliers

---

### How do I do it?

↦ Define and document requirements to be met by suppliers

↦ Evaluate suppliers' ability to meet requirements

↦ Develop mutual trust, respect, and commitment to customer satisfaction among organization and suppliers

↦ Integrate key elements of your organization's QMS with suppliers' quality improvement processes

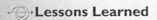

## Lessons Learned

Most organizations will find that adopting ISO 9001:2008 helps them:

↦ Gain a more complete systems understanding of all processes–from planning undertaken to be able to meet customer needs, through internal organization processes that actually meet those needs, and, eventually, to how organizational needs are expressed to your suppliers

↦ Identify opportunities for process improvement.

An effective approach to getting ready for ISO 9001 adoption is to follow the Plan—Do—Check—Act Cycle on page 45.

# Chapter

# THE PROCESS APPROACH

The Process Approach .............................. 16

Customer Oriented Processes (COPs) ............ 20

Identify Support and Management Processes ... 21

The Turtle Diagram ................................. 26

Terrapene™ ............................................ 27

Process Models ....................................... 29

Implementing the Process Approach
to a QMS (5 steps) ................................. 34

Questions for Management ......................... 37

Characteristics of a Process ....................... 38

ISO 9001 Process Flow Chart ...................... 41

Determining the appropriate amount
of documentation ..................................... 42

ISO 9001:2008 Helps Satisfy Internal
and External Customers............................. 43

Plan—Do—Check—Act .............................. 45

Difference Between Documents and Records .... 46

Quality Manual .......................................... 47

Preparing Quality Procedures........................ 49

Preparing Work/Job Instructions..................... 54

Preparing Other Documentation ................... 56

Improving Work Processes ........................... 58

Problem-Solving/Process-
Improvement Model.................................... 59

Flowcharting a Process .............................. 61

Process Control System ............................. 64

Control Chart............................................ 65

Process Capability .................................... 66

Collecting, Organizing, and Reporting
Data and Information ................................. 67

 **The Process Approach**

*First, read and understand how all the ISO 9001
requirements relate to your current processes.*

Your organization should describe the processes
by which it provides products and/or services to
an external customer(s). Once you have described
your processes, then tie the appropriate QMS requirements to a process. Some requirements may

apply to all processes. Some requirements may only be found to apply to one process. Within your processes, every requirement of ISO 9001 must be met for an organization to assert that it is following that standard.

### Checking off that all ISO 9001 requirements are being met is not sufficient

ISO 9001:2008 has an extensive list of requirements that describe a comprehensive QMS. All too often, at each stage of installation, operation, and verification of ISO 9001, a "checklist" approach has been followed during implementation and past audits. Confirmation in one or more documents that every element is being satisfactorily met has been taken as evidence that a functioning QMS is in operation. Unfortunately, this has led many to consider the process as a "paperwork" exercise with little relevance to how a product is made. Many actually see ISO compliance as a hindrance to getting work done. Another shortcoming of this "bottom up" approach is that users can overlook the need to observe, manage, and evaluate the total system from a management or, equally important, customer point of view. With this "checklist" approach, every tree may have been observed, with little or no assurance that they have been seen collectively as a forest. Another pitfall has been described as "silo" operation—viewing the relationship of components of the QMS as vertical rather than horizontal—with the risk of overlooking how the components relate, interact, and affect each other.

## Value of the Process Approach

The emphasis on the process approach transforms the QMS into a business model instead of a compliance model. Focusing on compliance only has resulted in a lot of wasted paper. Focusing on processes and the performance of the organization gives top management a useful tool for employing improvements in both customer satisfaction and organizational efficiencies. Some industries have provided excellent guidance on how to implement the process approach. Examples we will use in this book come from the aerospace and automotive industries.

ISO 9001 *does not prescribe how a process approach is to be implemented.*

It is up to the organization to determine methods of implementation and to be able to prove that implementation is effective for them and their customers. The process approach can best be understood by defining the QMS as a set of interrelated or interacting processes, with regard to both effectiveness and efficiency, which transform input into output.

The examples in this publication illustrate a process approach that focuses on "line of sight" to the customer. Each organization must describe its own unique processes...the way in which it produces a product and/or provides a service. Examples of process descriptions begin on page 29; however, the organization may use any method of process description.

Resist any pressure to follow a definitive, prescriptive way of describing your organization. **A definitive format is not required.** Refer to ISO 9001:2008, 0.1

General, first paragraph, third sentence: "*It is not the intent of this International Standard to imply uniformity in the structure of the QMS or uniformity of documentation.*"

*To provide an example of an acceptable approach, this publication offers the following descriptions:*

All processes follow the process approach described in 0.2 of the Standard. This shows that a process exists because of customer needs (input) that is fulfilled by the process meeting that need (output). Due to the great number of processes in any organization, some method of "grouping" or "classifying" processes is needed. One method to apply the process approach begins with those processes that address an external customer's needs first. These are defined as "Customer Oriented Processes" (COPs) See examples on page 20. Note that each meets an external customer's need, which is why they are important.

After identifying these COPs (sometimes referred to as "Main, Key, Core," or other such primary names), the organization would need to identify the processes by which the leadership manages the organization and the processes that are internal processes to the organization by which the organization is supported and maintained. Again, none of these names are specified. These are only examples of possible names. The important focus of this process identification is to identify what your organization actually does, not to try to use some name or names of processes that do not reflect your organization's reality.

## Customer Oriented Processes (COPs) Examples:

**Market Analysis/Customer Requirements** (customer needs you to know their requirements…you know their requirements)

**Bid/Tender** (customer needs a bid to be tendered…the bid is tendered)

**Order/Contract** (customer needs to place an order…an order is placed)

**Product and Process Design** (customer needs the product and process to be designed…the product and process are designed)

**Product and Process Verification/Validation** (customer needs the product and process design(s) to be verified/validated…the product and process design(s) is (are) verified/validated)

**Product Production** (customer needs for product to be produced…product is produced)

**Delivery** (customer needs for the product to be delivered…product is delivered)

**Payment** (customer needs to pay…has paid)

**Warranty/Service** (customer needs warranty or service concerns addressed…warranty or service concerns are addressed)

**Post Sales/Customer Feedback** (customer needs feedback to be heard…feedback is received by the organization)

# Identify Support and Management Processes

In addition to key processes, organizations normally require that a number of "support and management processes" be in place and functioning. These are in addition to the realization of products and services.

### *Examples of possible management processes:*

- Management planning (business planning)
- Management review
- Analysis of data
- Continual improvement
- Corrective and preventive action
- Record keeping
- Document and data control
- Internal auditing

### *Examples of possible supporting processes:*

- Training
- Housekeeping
- Maintenance of facility
- Maintenance of equipment
- Computer maintenance, upgrading, and repair

Support and management processes are as important as production processes. Each should be identified and described so that their operations can be understood. Most support and management processes link to most or all of the other processes. For example, the support process for "record keeping" may occur in a number of different functions employed in the organization.

"Main" or "Core" or "COPs" are the first level of processes, and "Support" and/or "Management" processes may all have **sub-processes**. Sub-processes are simply component processes of the larger processes. Many organizations will identify processes and sub-processes until a procedure or work instruction that defines the steps or activities that make up the process has been reached.

Interfaces and linkages between processes and relationships with the customer become apparent with the process approach. When defining a process, the organization should first define the external customer of that particular process. This allows the process to be defined as meeting a customer need.

- **Input:** the customer's need for that process to deliver a result. This need is defined in terms of specifications at the characteristic level. There may also be regulatory requirements associated with that need

  - By definition, in a COP process (could be called Main, Key, or Core) the organization's external customer defines the need

    - Delivery, for example, is defined by the customer's need for the product to be delivered. Requirements for delivery would be specified by the customer

- Production, for example, is defined by the customer's need for the product to be produced. Product production requirements would be specified by the customer and by the organization

➻ In a support and/or management process, the organization is the customer for that process

- In internal quality auditing, for example, the organization is the customer. The requirements for meeting that customer's need would be specified. This would include the organization's external customer's requirements for how that process was conducted, for organizational requirements, and for regulatory requirements

   - In training, for example, the organization is a customer of this process, as personnel in the organization require training

➻ **Output:** the need, stated in the terms of input, that is achieved

The following graphic illustrates this concept.

A process is a chain of value–added activities that conclude in a product or a service being delivered to a customer.

A process comes into existence to meet a customer need.

| INPUT | OUTPUT |
|---|---|
| **Customer's need** | **Customer's need is met** |
| (expressed in requirements at the characteristic level) | (the characteristic of the output meets the requirements) |

And a chain of activities between these two limits

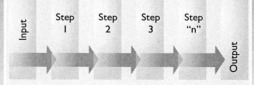

Input | Step 1 | Step 2 | Step 3 | Step "n" | Output

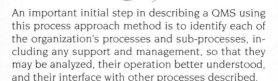

An important initial step in describing a QMS using this process approach method is to identify each of the organization's processes and sub-processes, including any support and management, so that they may be analyzed, their operation better understood, and their interface with other processes described.

*Tools to help identify and analyze processes*

A good place to start is with a "high level" flow chart of core processes. This can be made up of **turtles** that show the interactions of processes.

The **turtle** is a diagram format, shown on page 26, in which turtle parts represent the key elements of a process:

**The body**: process definition
   (The transformation activities of the process)

**The head**: input

**The tail**: output

**The four feet**: The four boxes are pulled from inside the process and help you see what is going on inside the process activities. Each of these boxes are interrelated to each of the other four boxes.

Example of a Turtle Diagram
*This is not a required tool and, if used, the format is not specified*

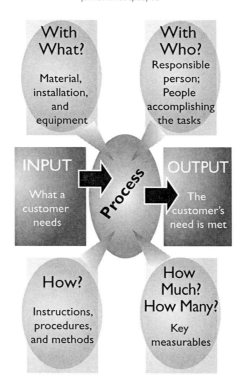

The turtle aids in the definition of processes, sub-processes, management, and support processes, and provides a convenient way to demonstrate interfaces between processes.

## Terrapene™

This is an example of a software program that uses the turtle methodology.

It helps a user in developing a visual model of each individual process—a visual model, which clearly illustrates the process's resources, responsibilities, measurements, product realization, input, and output. Overall, Terrapene assists organizations to identify and define the layers of interlinked "core" and "support" processes and enables auditors and management to quickly focus on gaps and improvements. See page 28 for a Terrapene window with one selected process for further analysis; visit www.terrapeneintl.com for additional information and examples.

Select a Process

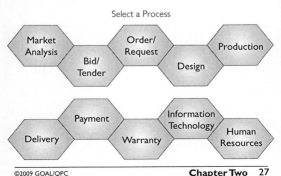

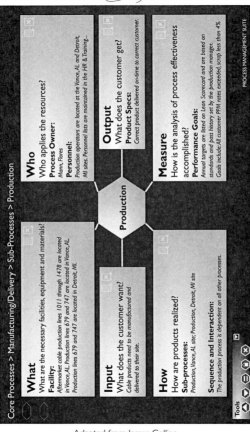

Core Processes > Manufacturing/Delivery > Sub-Processes > Production

## What
What are the necessary facilities, equipment and materials?

**Facility:**
Aftermarket cable production lines 1011 through 1478 are located in Vance, AL. Production lines 679 and 747 are located in Vance, AL. Production lines 679 and 747 are located in Detroit, MI.

## Input
What does the customer want?
Cable products need to be manufactured and delivered to their site.

## How
How are products realized?

**Sub-processes:**
Production, Vance, AL site; Production, Detroit, MI site

**Sequence and Interaction:**
The production process is dependent on all other processes.

## Who
Who applies the resources?

**Process Owner:**
Mann, Flores

**Personnel:**
Production operators are located at the Vance, AL and Detroit, MI sites. Personnel lists are maintained in the HR & Training...

## Output
What does the customer get?

**Product Specs:**
Correct product delivered on-time to correct customer.

## Measure
How is the analysis of process effectiveness accomplished?

**Performance Goals:**
Annual targets are listed on Lean Scorecard and are based on standards and past history set by the production manager. Goals include: All customer PPM rates exceeded; scrap less than 4%

Production

PROCESS MANAGEMENT SUITE

Tools

Adapted from James Collins,
Plexus International, Inc., Minneapolis, MN

The Memory Jogger™ 9001:2008 | ©2009 GOAL/QPC

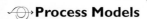

# Process Models

### *What is a model?*

A model is a generalized method describing the sequence and interactions of related actions that result in an output. The model can be written to describe either the current or future state of the management system processes.

### *Why use a model?*

A Process model can help you gain an understanding of the management system processes and how they either add to or detract from customer value. Additionally, to be fully useful, the model must also be able to illustrate not only linear but concurrent relationships, and the resulting transformation of input to output. A process model allows the organization to understand itself more readily and makes its process more transparent and more easily understood. It is important for the organization to choose a model that truly helps it explain what it does and whom it serves.

**Some examples of process models** are provided here that might be used to identify key processes, their sequence, and interaction.

➡ Octopus model, a literal application of the process approach methodology using Customer Oriented Processes (COPs). See pages 20 and 30

➡ Core Process Mapping, using the Advanced Product Quality Planning (APQP) model, an Automotive Core Tool, as a primary process model. See page 31

◆◆ Value stream model, a tool that draws a visual portrayal of each process in the flow of material and information. This is often referred to as "Lean." See page 32

◆◆ IDEF0, a Structured Analysis Design Technique, which illustrates all system data and activities, their intra-process relationships (linkages), inputs, outputs, controls (requirements), and mechanisms (people and infrastructure)

## The octopus is a single concept process model based on Customer Oriented Processes (COPs)

See page 20 for a detailed description of each of the 10 COPs illustrated in this octopus.

# Core Process Mapping
(*Advanced Product Quality Planning*)

## Core Processes

| Input Output | Engineering · Purchasing · Manufacturing · Sales · Quality · Shipping · Marketing | |
|---|---|---|
| Customer Expectations/ Specifications | Planning | Product Assurance Plan |
| Approved Product Assurance Plan | Product Design | Engineering Drawings and Specifications |
| Approved Engineering Design | Process Design | Process Capability Studies |
| Process Requirements/ Changes | Validation | Production Part Approval |
| Approved Production Part Plan | Production/Delivery | Product or Service |
| Returns Complaints and Surveys | Feedback/Correction | Corrections to Product, Process, and System |

## *Value Stream Mapping*

The term *value stream* refers to all the activities a company must perform to design, order, produce, and deliver its products or services to customers. A value stream has three main parts:

- ‣ The flow of materials, from receipt from suppliers to delivery to customers

- ‣ The transformation of raw materials into finished goods

- ‣ The flow of information that supports and directs both the flow of materials and the transformation of raw materials into finished goods

Several value streams are often operating within a company; value streams can also involve more than one company.

A manufacturer's enterprise value stream includes all actions required to bring a product through the main flows essential to every product. Each action is either value adding (machining performed, heat-treated, plated, painted, etc.) or non-value adding (sitting in a bin waiting for an activity to be performed). Looking at your manufacturing processes from a value stream perspective means looking at the larger process and how they interrelate—the forest, not the individual trees. It means paying attention to improving the system as a whole, beginning to end, rather than focusing on individual processes.

Value stream mapping can be a simple or complex tool that draws a visual portrayal of each process in the flow of material and information.

## Sample Value Stream Map

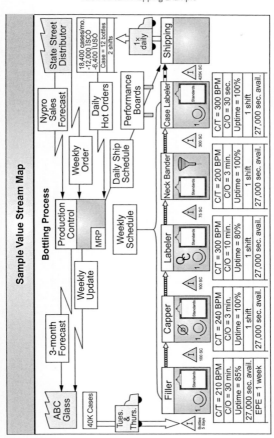

# Implementing the Process Approach to a QMS

## Preparation stage

Become familiar with existing/new QMS requirements of ISO 9001:2008 and provide training, as needed, within the organization. Identify the requirements that your product/service is to meet, as established by your organization, customers, suppliers, and statutory and regulatory requirements.

- Demonstrate understanding of the new approach

- Ensure top management understanding, involvement, and support

- Form implementation team(s) of qualified people from various levels of management and operations

## Step 1. Analyze the organization's system: "Find the processes"

Using the turtle analytical tool, identify, define, and understand all of the main processes needed for the QMS, the sequences and interaction of processes and the input, transformation, and output for each process, including contact with the customer.

- Measure, monitor, analyze and determine the effectiveness and efficiency of processes

- Consider use of Terrapene software to aid in identification of main processes

## Step 2. Define the system's (single concept) model, based on work from Step 1

- ➔ Octopus with turtles
- ➔ Core Process Mapping, using the APQP model
- ➔ Value stream maps
- ➔ IDEF0 Process Modeling Technique
- ➔ Any other appropriate process tools; text only may be used, but becomes very confusing and hard to follow for most readers when describing the organization's processes

## Step 3. Define the support and management processes

Using the turtle analytical tool, identify, define, and understand:

- ➔ Support and management processes
- ➔ The sequence and interaction of support and management processes and sub-processes
- ➔ Input and output for each process, including contact with the customer
- ➔ Internal audit planning and execution
- ➔ Use flow charts to study existing processes

## Step 4. Adequately define and communicate the QMS

Confirm that the QMS is focused on the performance of the system as it meets customer needs and expectations.

Standardize communication of information needed to ensure operation, control, and records. Identify existence of over-documentation that serves little purpose in assuring customer satisfaction. Simplify, combine, or even eliminate documentation (including procedures) while meeting requirements that describe processes identified in steps 2 and 3.

Capture simplified processes in concise documentation that is easily understood by everyone.

Ensure that the implementation of your QMS meets the requirements of your customer and of the Standard. *Note that you define your actual process, then link the requirements of the customer and the standard to your processes.*

### Step 5. Align first-party and third-party QMS audits by standardizing the analytic and communication tools

Provide for internal auditing of all processes, with a focus on performance, while checking for compliance and continuous improvement opportunities.

Establish a standard process for planning, executing, and reporting the results of all organizational audits (i.e., system, product, process).

Define the need for, and potential value of, QMS third-party registration.

### Follow-up stage

Demonstrate assurance, organizational efficiency, effectiveness, and continuous improvement from the QMS.

Continually enhance top management support and commitment to provide needed resources (competent people and capable infrastructure).

Evaluate changes resulting from continual improvement efforts. Repeat comprehensive analysis of all activities periodically to continue improvement in output quality and productivity.

Identify requirements that your product/service are to meet, as established by your organization, customers, and statutory and regulatory requirements.

Monitor and measure, as appropriate, your processes to ensure the processes are under control. A predictable, stable outcome is the goal of process control.

## Questions which directly drive management decisions in a process-based organization

- What are the requirements (input)?
- What is to be delivered (output)?
- With what (equipment, installations)?
- With whom (training, knowledge, skills)?
- How many/how much (key measurables)?
- How (instructions, procedures, methods)?
- Why are the strategic and tactical goals important (objectives)?

## Questions that executives must answer—and can—with a process-based system

- How do I invest in my business?

- How do I invest in my product or service?

- How do I sell more products or services—and gain more market share?

- How do I fulfill existing commitments?

- What do my customers think of my product?

- How do I serve my customers, suppliers, and employees?

## Characteristics of a process

- Has an owner

- Is defined

- Is normally documented

- Linkages are established

- Is monitored and measured

- Has records maintained

## Support process questions related to risk

- With what (materials, equipment)?

- With who (skills, training)?

- With what key criteria (measurement, assessment)?

- How (methods, techniques, standardized work)?

### "Ingredients" of a process

A process owner, who:

•• Has the responsibility and authority (assumed or is given) for effective process operation

•• Defines expectations of the process

•• Assures competent personnel

### Input
What the customer needs

### A chain of activities
•• Identification of what the process does

•• Production/realization of a product or service

### Output
What the process delivers; fulfillment of the need identified in the input

### Measurement of key factors
Quantifies process performance in the context of added value, effectiveness, and efficiency

### Procedures and work instructions
How the activities are accomplished and the output delivered

### What does it mean for me?
ISO 9001:2008 is about knowing and understanding your customers (both internal and external) and their requirements, and then understanding the

---

audit process to ensure that your day-to-day activities meet those requirements.

The work you do has a number of steps that must be done to provide a product or service. Other people also perform tasks that affect your work. This may include providing the parts or services you need. The process approach helps everyone understand these activities and the linking processes to better manage a system that helps you accomplish your work. It is intended to be a practical tool, not simply a paperwork exercise that actually gets in your way.

As your organization gets involved in implementing ISO 9001:2008, you may be asked to:

- Participate, or assist, in identifying how the work that you do that affects the quality of the products or services your organization provides to customer(s)
- Improve your work processes
- Write procedures or work instructions that describe your work
- Keep records and data
- Participate in internal audits
- Participate in ongoing process improvement
- Participate in external registration and surveillance audits if your organization seeks registration

To understand the sequencing and activities that you will need to undertake, follow the ISO 9001:2008 implementation flow chart on page 41.

ISO 9001 Process Flow Chart

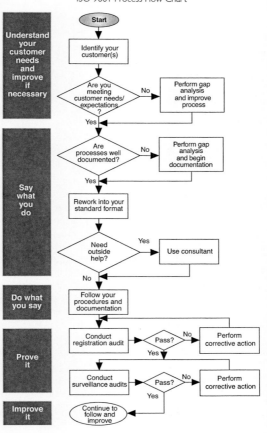

**Understand your customer needs and improve if necessary**

Start

Identify your customer(s)

Are you meeting customer needs/expectations? → No → Perform gap analysis and improve process

Yes

**Say what you do**

Are processes well documented? → No → Perform gap analysis and begin documentation

Yes

Rework into your standard format

Need outside help? → Yes → Use consultant

No

**Do what you say**

Follow your procedures and documentation

**Prove it**

Conduct registration audit → Pass? → No → Perform corrective action

Yes

Conduct surveillance audits → Pass? → No → Perform corrective action

Yes

**Improve it**

Continue to follow and improve

# Determining the appropriate amount of documentation

ISO 9001:2008 is very specific as to the need for documentation sufficient to demonstrate that requirements of the Standard have been met. Organizations should take care to ensure that these stated documentation requirements continue to be followed. The process for auditing the business management system practices to search out where required documentation is not being followed is called **gap analysis**. As gaps are discovered, obvious corrective action is put into practice to fully meet documentation requirements, and to assure that a gap does not recur in the future.

However, just as much attention should be given to avoiding **over-documentation**, the practice of maintaining documents that are not required by the Standard, and which do not add value. These may include practices that were once in use, but are no longer needed. The Process Approach emphasizes the need for identifying and eliminating unneeded documentation. Actively searching out ways to reduce unneeded recorded information parallels the technique of lean enterprise as it applies to manufactured product eliminating those activities that do not serve the objectives of the organization sufficiently to justify their existence.

The goal should be to optimize documentation levels to a level appropriate to the needs of the organization, and to continually reduce documentation as your need for it diminishes.

# ⊙ ISO 9001:2008 Helps Satisfy Internal and External Customers

•▸ The business enterprise needed to consistently produce a product or service in compliance with all customer requirements

•▸ The need to prevent all product or service defects, and to reduce variation and waste in the total supply chain

•▸ The need to ensure the direct leadership of all top management in all organization activities

•▸ The need for competent personnel at all levels of the organization

•▸ The need for consistent process controls, standardized work practices, suitable production equipment, trustworthy measurement devices, and standardized system performance metrics

•▸ The need for well-trained and competent personnel to support an aggressive internal audit process

•▸ The need for direct top management accountability in the strategic and tactical management of the business enterprise

•▸ The need for an improvement culture with direct contribution of all organizational personnel, from top management to the production equipment operator

ISO 9001 Helps Satisfy
Internal and External Customers

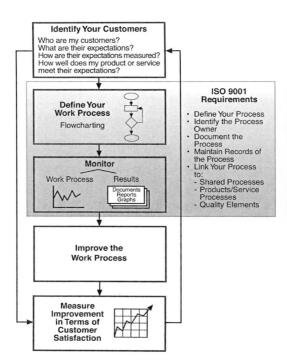

**Identify Your Customers**

Who are my customers?
What are their expectations?
How are their expectations measured?
How well does my product or service
meet their expectations?

**Define Your Work Process**

Flowcharting

**Monitor**

Work Process          Results

Documents
Reports
Graphs

**Improve the Work Process**

**Measure Improvement in Terms of Customer Satisfaction**

**ISO 9001 Requirements**

- Define Your Process
- Identify the Process Owner
- Document the Process
- Maintain Records of the Process
- Link Your Process to:
  - Shared Processes
  - Products/Service Processes
  - Quality Elements

Information provided courtesy of William Howarth,
D.B. Riley, Inc., Worcester, MA

# ⟨⊙⟩ PLAN—DO—CHECK—ACT

A key to getting ready for ISO 9001 registration is to follow the sequence of the Plan-Do-Check-Act (PDCA) Cycle. Each step can follow the PDCA Cycle: documentation, the process-improvement model (see page 59) and, where called for, a registration audit and surveillance audits.

Because it is a continual cycle, it is sometimes appropriate to start at "Check" for a Check—Act—Plan—Do Cycle. The QMS documentation process would then follow this sequence:

**CHECK** Understand the contents of the Standard and assess organizational performance

**ACT** Determine the need for system improvement before preparing documentation for ISO 9001:2008 registration

**PLAN** Establish a schedule for training and development of process descriptions or review of existing process descriptions

**DO** Document the QMS sufficiently to be able to demonstrate its operation to the organization's top management, process owners, and eventually to a third-party registrar

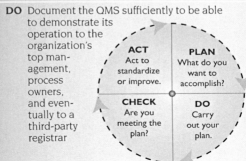

# ⟨◯⟩ The Difference Between Documents and Records

ISO 9001:2008 defines a record as a "special type of document…"

ISO 9000:2005 defines a record as a:

> document stating results achieved or providing evidence of activities performed

> Note
> Records can be used, for example, to document **traceability** and to provide evidence of verification, **preventive action,** and **corrective action**.

The practical use of documents and records merits further explanation.

**Documents,** in ISO 9001:2008 usage, are causative, and generally consist of permanent documentation describing or defining systems, processes, procedures, and products. Examples include product specifications and quality manuals. Documents are generally being used at present, but may become records when they are no longer current or have been used (a form is typically a document until it is filled out; then it is a record of what was captured on the form).

**Records** provide current and historic evidence of activities conducted. They are reports of results achieved, or evidence of activities performed at a given time. Examples include inspection and test records, records confirming traceability, evidence of verification, or preventive and corrective actions.

# Quality Manual

## *Preparing the Quality Manual*

The Quality Manual is the top level of your organization's documentation system. It typically states your organization's policy on, and commitment to, customer satisfaction; however, these items may be covered in a separate document.

The Quality Manual *must* include the boundaries (scope) of your organization that are covered by the manual and *must* include details of any exclusion you are claiming to the requirements of the Standard.

The quality manual could be used to provide the index for documentation, including organizational procedures and, as appropriate, job instructions.

The body of the quality manual must include the procedures required by the Standard or make reference to where they can be found.

The primary purpose of the Quality Manual is the understanding of your QMS and the clear understanding of what your organization's processes are and how they interact and link to each other by textual or process map description. The quality manual is a "40,000 foot view" of your organization and what it exists to do. This paraphrasing of the entire QMS by a process approach is outlined in Section 0.2 and the requirements found in Section 4.1 of the Standard.

## Sample Outline of a Quality Manual

- ✦ Quality Policy

- ✦ Overview of the organization covered by the manual, including a Process "map" that provides a high-level view of your organization and shows its sequence and interactions. Examples include the octopus with turtles, value-stream maps, flow charts, IDEF0 multi-layered process maps, *or* any other appropriate tools or combinations thereof.

- ✦ Distribution List of Controlled Copies

- ✦ Procedures Index (included or referenced)

- ✦ Forms Index (included or referenced)

See ISO/TR 10013:2001, "Guidelines for QMS Documentation," for guidance in developing a quality manual. There is no required format for a Quality Manual and each organization may develop one that uniquely meets its own organization's needs, as long as it minimally covers the three required sub-clauses in ISO 9001:2008 4.2.2: scope, procedures, and interactions.

If you used the recommended approach shown in the first section of this chapter, you could use the process map and associated turtles as your Quality Manual.

# ⊙ Preparing Quality Procedures

Procedures are the documents defining who, what, when, and where policies are carried out. Normally written by the process owners, they describe the activities that accomplish the output of the identified process and their relation to the organization operations as a whole. You will, more than likely, participate in the preparation of your procedures and/or work/job instructions. A sequence for developing business system procedures appears on page 50.

### Possible Outline of a Quality (Business System) Procedure

- ◆ **Purpose/Objective:** aim of the procedure

- ◆ **Scope:** what the procedure does and does not cover

- ◆ **Responsibilities:** who (by job function) has responsibilities for specific tasks or actions

- ◆ **References:** to all documents covered under the procedure

- ◆ **Definitions:** of key terms or acronyms

- ◆ **Procedures:** description of the actions or tasks to be carried out, by whom, and in what sequence

- ◆ **Documentation:** what documentation and records are needed

*The turtle diagram or a multi-layer process map such as IDEF0, discussed previously, may also serve as a procedural format.*

## Quality Procedure Writing Process Flow Chart

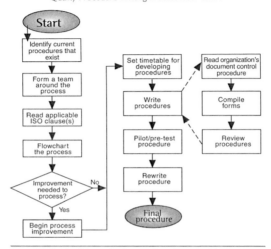

## Medication Dispensing Process Flow Chart for Nursing

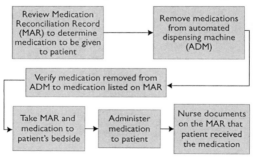

# Suggestions for Writing Documentation

Procedures, Work/Job Instructions, and Other Documentation

## Document The Process

- Keep it short and simple. Don't over-document
    - Flowchart the process, if appropriate. Make extensive use of charts and tables
    - Use a standardized format
    - Keep the audience in mind:
        - Make the meaning very clear; have someone else read it and explain back what you said
        - Make the text grammatically correct
        - Search out errors in spelling and punctuation
        - Avoid jargon

*Continued on next page*

- Separate ideas into individual sentences or paragraphs
- Write to the task, not an individual; documents are written to help workers perform their tasks more efficiently and consistently
- Ask the user to help write the documentation

↦ For every task, identify:
  - Who is responsible for ensuring that it is done?
  - Standards to be met/completion criteria
  - What resources are needed?
  - What records are kept?
  - What to do if it doesn't work

↦ Pre-test procedures. Have those who will use the procedures try them and provide feedback

# Document Control Procedure

**Purpose**
This document describes the procedure to be followed for the approval, issue, and maintenance of all controlled documentation.

**Scope**
This procedure shall apply to all controlled documentation relating to all company products and services.

**References**
Document Change Procedure DOC-PROC-001
Document Register DOC-REG-001

**Procedure**
All controlled documentation shall be subject to approval by the following before issue and release:
   a) Originator
   b) Originator's manager
   c) Quality manager

Released documentation can only be changed in accordance with the Change Control System DOC-PROC-001.

A record of all controlled documentation shall be maintained by the quality manager indicating the following:
   a) Reference number
   b) Issue number
   c) Disposition of copies

Details of controlled document holders shall be held on the Document Register.

Officially distributed copies of the documents shall be identified by a red "Official Distribution" stamp giving date of distribution. Action affecting product quality shall only be taken on the basis of information contained in officially distributed copies of controlled documents.

Master copies of all controlled documentation shall be held by the quality manager.

All copies of documentation that become obsolete by reissue shall be promptly removed from distribution. One copy shall be archived by the quality manager; all other copies shall be destroyed.

From *The ISO 9000 Handbook*, Irwin Professional Publishing, Chapter 7, Quality System Documentation, p. 239. Reproduced with permission of The McGraw-Hill Companies.

# Preparing Work/Job Instructions

Work or job instructions are documentation that describes how work is accomplished and are usually written by the operators and documentation facilitators. You will probably find that you already have instructions for many of your key operations.

Follow the directions for writing documentation listed on pages 51–52. Use the following list of points when you are documenting your work.

## Work/Job Instructions

- Start from existing written work/job instructions
- Use a team approach in preparing instructions
- Verify that existing instructions describe the present activity; if not, correct them
- Determine whether present practices are satisfactory or if a quality improvement process should be followed
- Adopt improved practice, if necessary
- Complete a turtle, flow chart or process map of complex operations
- Begin upgrading and evaluating the job instructions
- Verify that the work/job instructions are being followed as the work/job is being completed
- Use work/job instructions as a basis for training

(a) → **Tank Car Wash Rack and Inspection**

(b) **Document no.:** TKWR02 | **Description:** Tank car wash and inspection

(c) **Revision no.:** 0 | **Sheet:** 1 of 3 ← (d)

(g) **Prepared by:** Paul Brown | **Approved by:** T. Jones ← (f)

**Issued by:** Cleaning Section | **Issue Date:** May 31, 2009 ← (e)

### 1.0 Introduction

Prior to loading, most tank cars are washed and internally and externally inspected. Cars that are recycled for specified products are not washed. These recycled tanks are controlled by the shipping services supervisor.

### 2.0 Preparation

1. Switching crew selects tank car.
2. Secure tank car by chock and hand brakes.
3. Connect ground cables to each car.
4. Attach safety appliances to each car.
5. Depressurize all pressurized tanks.
6. Manway bottom outlet valves.
7. Open: Secondary valves
   Vent valves
   Induction valves.
8. Remove cap from bottom outlet valve nozzle.

A "controlled document" will have:

(a) Title
(b) Document number (a unique identifier)
(c) Revision indicator (e.g., Rev. A, -001, B)
(d) Page number (e.g., Page 1 of 3, Page 1.2, 1-2.3)
(e) Date issued/revised (e.g., April 6, 2009 4/6/09)
(f) Approval (the approving authority by signature and perhaps also position title)
(g) Prepared by/Issued by (name, position, and/or department)

---

Reprinted from *ISO 9000: Preparing for Registration*, James L. Lamprecht, by courtesy of Marcel Dekker, NY

# Preparing Other Documentation

The Standard requires that organizations identify "documents needed by the organization to ensure the effective planning, operation and control of its processes." This might include documents like your business plan, drawings, and control plans. Your documentation must include all documents used by the organization to make products and provide services to your customers. It would also include all forms, or controlled documents (hard copy and/or electronic) that become records. Compilation of a current file of these forms involves middle managers and quality managers.

### Examples of Other Documents

Quality Objectives and Commitment
Quality Policy
Organization Chart
New Employee Orientation
Certificate of Training

Design Requirements
Bill of Design
Bill of Materials
Bill of Process
Supplier Review
Purchase Order
Receiving Record

Build Forecasts/Schedules
Statutory / Regulatory Records
Hazardous Materials Records
Transportation Records

Product Release Stamp
Storage Assessment
Repair Order Form

Discrepancy Report
Major Customer Forecast

Phoned-In Sales Order
Customer Orders

Warranty and Repair Tag
Repair/Warranty Log
Returned Product Authorizations

Internal Quality Audit Records
Maintenance Work Orders
Process Studies
Measurement System Studies
Measurement System Calibration Records

# Improving Work Processes

Continual improvement should be a constant goal. Opportunities for corrective action and for improvement might be necessary if you:

- ➻ Are not meeting your customer needs and requirements
- ➻ Have not satisfied the requirements of the registration or surveillance audits
- ➻ Are seeking to reduce process variation and waste

### Problem-Solving/Process-Improvement Model

A systematic approach to focus on a problem, identify root cause(s), and develop and implement solutions and action plans.

### Flowcharting a Process

A graphic tool for documenting and understanding the flow or sequence of events in your work process.

### Process Mapping

A mapping tool that defines both current and future state of business system processes by emphasizing inputs, outputs, controls, and mechanisms.

### Process Control System

The use of data as feedback on how a process is performing.

### Collecting, Organizing, and Reporting Data and Information

In problem solving/process improvement, controlled documentation, and record keeping, you will need to understand some basic points on collecting data and how best to present the data graphically.

Note:
*Also see ISO 10004: "Guidelines for Quality Improvement."*

# Problem-Solving/Process-Improvement Model

There are many standard models for making improvements. They all attempt to provide a repeatable set of steps that a team or individual can learn and follow. The improvement storyboard is only one of many models that include typical steps using typical tools. Follow this model or any other model that creates a common language for continuous improvement within your organization. The PDCA model is repeated here from page 45 as an example of a problem-solving/process-improvement model.

## 🎵 Plan

1. Select the problem/process that will be addressed first (or next) and describe the improvement opportunity.

2. Describe the current process surrounding the improvement opportunity.

3. Describe all of the possible causes of the problem and agree on the root cause(s).

4. Develop an effective and workable solution and action plan, including targets for improvement.

## 🎵 Do

5. Implement the solution or process change.

## 🎵 Check

6. Review and evaluate (measure and analyze) the result of the change.

## 🎵 Act

7. Reflect and act on learning.

PDCA from *The Memory Jogger™ II*, GOAL/QPC
See *The Problem Solving Memory Jogger™* from GOAL/QPC
for more detail on problem solving/process improvement.

# Flowcharting a Process

Flowcharting allows you or a team to identify the actual flow or sequence of events in a process that any product or service follows. A flow chart helps uncover unexpected complexity in the process, allowing you to understand the actual process steps, and then work to identify improvement opportunities where additional data can be collected and investigated.

 *How do I do it?*

1. **Determine the frame or boundaries of the process.**

    ◆◆ Clearly define the start and end (scope) of the process

    ◆◆ Determine the level of detail needed to clearly understand the process and identify problem areas

2. **Determine the steps in the process.**

    ◆◆ Brainstorm a list of all major activities, inputs, outputs, and decisions from the beginning to the end of the process

3. **Sequence the steps.**

    ◆◆ Arrange the steps in the order in which they are carried out

    ◆◆ Unless flowcharting a new process, sequence what is, not what "should be"

    ◆◆ Look for what activities are sequential and concurrent. This determines the correct flow

4. **Draw the flow chart using the appropriate symbols** (*see chart on page 63*).

   ↦ Keep it simple and consistent in the amount of detail shown

   ↦ Label each process step using words that everyone understands

5. **Test the flow chart for completeness.**

   ↦ Are the symbols used correctly?

   ↦ Are the process steps identified clearly?

   ↦ Make sure every feedback loop is closed

   ↦ Check that every continuation point has a corresponding point elsewhere

   ↦ Use only one arrow out of an activity box. If there is more than one arrow, you may need to add a decision diamond

   ↦ Validate the flow chart with people who carry out the process actions

6. **Finalize the flow chart.**

   ↦ Is the process being run the way it should be?

   ↦ Are people following the process as charted?

   ↦ Are there obvious complexities or redundancies that can be reduced or eliminated?

   ↦ How different is the current process from ideal? Draw an ideal flow chart and compare the two to identify discrepancies and opportunities for improvements

✍ *See The Memory Jogger™ II for more detail on construction and interpretation of flow charts.*

Flow Chart Symbols

| Symbol | Represents | Detail/Example |
|---|---|---|
| (oval) | Start/End Input/Output | Request for proposal Request for new hire, raw material |
| (square) | Task, action, execution point | Hold a meeting Make a phone call Open a box |
| (diamond) ? No / Yes | Decision point | Yes/no Accept/reject Pass/fail Criteria met/not met |
| (document shape) | Document | Fill out a report or a form, Job request Meeting minutes |
| (shadowed box) | Shadow signifies additional flow chart for this task | There are no subtasks for this major task study Subtasks not included due to limited space |
| (D shape) | Delay | Waiting for service Report sitting on a desk |
| →(A) (A)→ | Continuation | Go to another page Go to another part of the chart |
| → | Arrow | Shows direction or flow of the process steps |

From GOAL/QPC's *Coach's Guide to The Memory Jogger™ II*

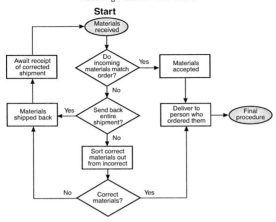

## ⬲ Process Control System

A process control system is the continuous cycle of using data as feedback on the performance of a process to identify sources of variation and waste, and then working to reduce or eliminate these sources. Doing so results in improved outputs that better meet your customers' defined quality of product and service.

All work that we do is a process. There are definable inputs, steps, and decisions that produce outputs of products and services for our customers. Unfortunately, no two outputs are exactly alike. They vary from each other because of variations of the inputs: people, equipment, materials, methods, and environment.

Sources of variation can be grouped into two major classes:

- ➤➤ **Common cause:** Always present—part of the random variation inherent in the process itself. Its origin can usually be traced to an element of the process that only management can correct; it is beyond the control of the operator

- ➤➤ **Special cause:** Intermittent, localized, seasonal, unpredictable, or unstable. Its origin can usually be traced to an element of the system that can be corrected locally: that is, an employee or operator may be able to correct a special cause

Control charts help separate out these two sources of variation and identify who has responsibility for correcting them: management (common cause) or local operators, suppliers, machines, equipment, etc. (special cause).

## Control Chart

A control chart is a graphical tool that allows you to "visibly track" variation in a process over time. It is important to monitor changes in process variation to control the process. A process must be in statistical control before you can improve it.

A process is said to be in a state of statistical control, or "in control," when measurements from the process vary randomly within statistically calculated limits. That is, there are no points outside the limits and no points forming trend lines, shifts, cycles, or other patterns. Over time, the variation present is consistent and predictable.

A process that consistently and predictably produces product or service within three standard deviations, or +/- 3 sigma or 6 sigma (the statistically calculated "control limits"), of the mean is considered to be in a state of statistical control. This means that all special causes of variation within the process have been removed.

Note that a process that is "in control" may not be producing good product or service; however, it is consistent and predictable. It could be consistently and predictably bad!

Simple Control Chart

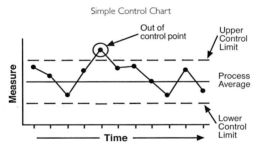

## Process Capability

Process capability is used to determine whether a process, given its natural variation, is capable of meeting established customer requirements or specifications. It helps you answer the questions "Is the process capable of meeting the requirement?", "Has there been a change in the process?," and "What percentage of my product or service is not meeting the customer requirement?"

Capability indices have been developed to compare the distribution of your process in relation to the customer specification limits. Before capability can be determined, a stable process must be obtained. A stable process can be represented by a measure of its variation—six standard (six sigma) deviations. Comparing six standard deviations of the process variation to the customer specification provides a measure of capability. Some measures of capability include Cp (simple) and its inverse Cr, Cpl, Cpu for single-sided specification limits, and Cpk (uses $3\hat{\sigma}$) for two-sided specification limits.

Calculation, construction, and interpretation of control charts and process capability are beyond the scope of this pocket guide. For more detailed information, see *The Memory Jogger*™ II, *The Fundamental Statistical Process Control Reference Manual* by the automotive Big Three (DaimlerChrysler, Ford, and General Motors), and *Understanding Variation* by Dr. Donald Wheeler. For more advanced techniques, see *Implementing Six Sigma* by Forrest Breyfogle. The five customer reference manuals referred to in ISO/TS 16949 are described on page 247.

## ⟿ Collecting, Organizing, and Reporting Data and Information

As you become involved in implementing your QMS, one of your responsibilities may include collecting, organizing, and reporting data and information about your work/process. Data and information are collected to document a current situation, as well as to understand how the process is performing and what action needs to be taken to control, fix, or improve it.

### Collecting data

- ✦ Clarify the purpose of the problem and focus only on what you need or what's required

- ✦ Make sure the data represent the process. Know what type of data or information you have; the data will often dictate the tool you will use or the way to display it

- ✦ Stratify data if necessary, e.g., separate it by days, machines, types, etc.

- ✦ Keep data collection and information forms simple

- ✦ Use historical data first, if available. This will set a baseline of past performance

### Organizing/reporting data and information

The tool you should use to organize and report data depends on the type of data you have or plan to collect; data can be words or numbers, and either counted or measured. Use the Tool and Data Chart on the following page to help you decide on the most appropriate tool.

### Statistical data

Predictable patterns or distributions of data can be described with statistics. These include:

- ✦ Measures of location (mean, median, mode)

- ✦ Measures of variation (range, standard deviation)

| Number Data (Count or attribute) | Tool to Use |
| --- | --- |
| • Show frequency of events | • Check Sheet<br>• Pareto |
| • Show process performance over time | • Run Chart<br>• Control Chart |
| • Show capability of process to meet customer requirements | • Process Capability |

| Number Data (Measure or variable) | Tool to Use |
| --- | --- |
| • Show relations among multiple data sets over time | • Radar Chart<br>• Run Chart |
| • Show centering and variation of a process | • Histogram |
| • Show correlations between two or more data sets | • Scatter |
| • Show process performance over time | • Run Chart<br>• Control Chart |
| • Show capability of process to meet customer requirements | • Process Capability |

✍️ Refer to *The Memory Jogger*™ II, or other statistical books for guidance on selection, construction, and interpretation of the quality control and management and planning tools.

# Chapter
# THREE

## AUDITING AND REGISTRATION

Getting Ready for Auditing and Registration.... 72

Role of the Registrar ................................. 74

Selecting a Registrar ................................ 75

Role of the Consultant.............................. 76

The Registration Audit.............................. 78

Surveillance Audits .................................. 80

The ISO 9001:2008 Registration
Audit Preparation Checklist ........................ 82

Lessons Learned in Implementing ISO 9001:2008. 84

Summary of Content of ISO 9001:2008 .............85

ISO 9001:2008:2000 – A Brief Overview...............86

# Getting Ready for Auditing and Registration

While preparing for and going through registration, you'll likely work with many people, both inside and outside your organization. To make best use of everyone's expertise, to manage your time effectively with them, and to have good working relationships, it is important to understand everyone's part in the implementation and registration process.

### The roles and responsibilities of everyone in your organization include:

- Committing to, and supporting, the ISO 9001:2008 implementation effort

- Having a cooperative, positive attitude

- Communicating the status of the effort

- Enthusiastically understanding and supporting the value of registration

### Other Roles and Responsibilities

### Top Management

- Ensure commitment, which is mandatory to success

- Help develop and promote the organization's quality policy and objectives

- Help develop high-level processes

- Implement any necessary changes

- Review progress

- ◆ Provide resources
- ◆ Ensure attainment and sustainment of ISO 9001:2008 registration, if required

## Managers

- ◆ Ensure effectiveness and efficiency of quality systems within your area

## Staff/Associates/Line Personnel

- ◆ Provide input and verify that documented procedures are adequate and accurate
- ◆ Understand and use your work/job instructions
- ◆ Understand your organization's quality policy and how it applies to you
- ◆ Be familiar with the appropriate ISO 9001:2008 requirements
- ◆ Direct any questions to the implementation team, the ISO 9001:2008 coordinator, or your manager or supervisor

## ISO 9001:2008 Coordinator/ Implementation Team

- ◆ Coordinate the registration process
- ◆ Act as a task leader and technical resource
- ◆ Oversee training of all staff

- ◆ Identify and obtain required documentation
- ◆ Develop the format of the quality manual
- ◆ Evaluate the documentation for conformance to the Standard
- ◆ Monitor and provide counsel for interpretation
- ◆ Coordinate, lead, and participate in internal audits
- ◆ Chair regular ISO 9001:2008 progress review meetings
- ◆ Report progress to all levels of management

Adapted from Linda Johnson,
Allegro MicroSystems, Inc., Worcester, MA

## Role of the Registrar

Registrars (also called Certification Bodies or CBs) are independent companies authorized to evaluate the capability of your organization to meet ISO 9001:2008 requirements. Auditors, who are qualified individuals trained in the ISO 9001:2008 standards, come into your organization and validate that you satisfy (or "comply with") the requirements. They audit your organization for the initial registrations, and return periodically to confirm that you continue to comply with the requirements. These are called surveillance audits.

## Selecting a Registrar

- ◆ Make sure the registrar is accredited. If you will be operating in an international market, make sure the chosen registrar meets internationally accepted requirements

- ◆◆ Consider whether you need a registrar with expertise in a particular industry

- ◆◆ Determine if the registrar will be responsive to your needs

- ◆◆ What types of services does the registrar offer? Training courses? Tailored preliminary audits?

- ◆◆ What is the registrar's track record and reputation (i.e., referrals)?

- ◆◆ How does the registrar train and maintain consistency among its assessors (continuing professional development)?

- ◆◆ What costs are involved (initial and long term – rates and quoting)?

- ◆◆ How does the registrar respond to non-compliances (i.e., referrals)?

### Working with a Registrar/Auditor(s)

- ◆◆ **Dos**

  - ◆◆ Get to know them since they will be coming back periodically

  - ◆◆ Remember that, to the registrar, you are the customer

  - ◆◆ Respond efficiently and effectively to auditors' inquiries

  - ◆◆ Understand your processes, procedures, records, and data

- ► Go into a meeting with the auditor well prepared

- ► **Don'ts**
    - ► Look to the registrar for advice on how to fix a negative finding. Registrars are not to serve as consultants

    - ► Try to lead the auditor or control the audit

    - ► Be afraid to answer a question with "I don't know." However, do say that you will find the answer and get back to them as quickly as possible

    - ► Be evasive, uncooperative, or inconclusive

## Role of the Consultant

Many organizations achieve ISO 9001:2008 registration without using outside consultants; however, using one may be a good investment. With knowledge, field experience, and understanding of the ISO 9001:2008 standards, as well as your business and industry, they can be valuable resources. Consultants often help plan the implementation effort, conduct training, and assist you and your organization to prepare for an audit. Also, they can help you reach the point where the QMS becomes the way your organization does day-to-day business.

## Working with a Consultant

- ➤➤ Ask for help in understanding how to implement ISO 9001:2008; don't ask the consultant to do your job

- ➤➤ Ask questions to help clarify any misunderstandings you may have on any of the ISO 9001:2008 standards that apply to you

- ➤➤ Ask for pointers on writing your job description or documenting your process(es)

- ➤➤ Ask for advice on how to conduct yourself during an audit

- ➤➤ Ask for the role of top management in the registration process

# ⟨◉⟩ The Registration Audit

Audits are a way of obtaining objective feedback on how effective your QMS is: what's working well, what can be improved, and what isn't fulfilling your planned levels of performance.

- **Internal audits** are self-audits that help your organization's readiness for the external audit conducted by your chosen registrar, as well as the overall performance of your business management system. They determine where your organization needs more training, more practice, or where a process description may need to be revised and improved

- **Third-party audits** are when your chosen registrar officially comes in to verify that you conform to the ISO 9001:2008 standards

## *Prior to the Audit*

- Submit your quality manual and any other documents required by your registrar, in advance, if so requested by the registrar

- The first audit of your QMS is called a "Stage 1" audit. This includes the review of your documentation by the registrar and is done to determine the readiness of your system to be audited. No nonconformity is written during the Stage 1; it is only a yes or no decision as to your readiness to proceed to the Stage 2 audit

- Consider arranging for a pre-assessment. This is typically considered by your registrar but could be carried out by a different organization. If you use an organization other than your registrar, then the organization providing your pre-assessment offers suggestions on how to strengthen your system. Your registrar is not allowed to act as a consultant and offer specific suggestions to address the requirements of the Standard (see ISO/IEC 17021, Section 5.2); however, they may offer opportunities for improvement

- Work with your registrar to schedule the Stage 2 site audit

- Train all members of the organization on the benefits of the implementation of ISO 9001:2008 and why your organization is seeking this registration. Help them understand how the audit will proceed and what types of questions the auditors will be asking. The internal audits you have accomplished should prepare them to be audited and they should know how to provide objective evidence of your QMS

### During the Audit

- Auditors will meet first with top management to provide an overview of the registration event

- Auditors will then circulate throughout the organization to determine if your QMS is in accordance with the ISO 9001:2008

- Auditors will observe the operations and ask questions concerning the work/job: How are you doing it? Why are you doing it? Are you following the process you have documented?

- Respond to questions honestly. Don't mislead or give uninformed replies

- Make sure that you are following your process

### After the Audit

- Work with the auditor on all findings in a professional manner

- Address any noncompliances in a positive way, correcting them and reporting back to the auditor in a timely manner

- Review your successes when you receive your certificate

- Continue to review system performance and improve your quality system

### Surveillance Audits

ISO 9001:2008 registered systems require periodic surveillance to ensure that they continue to function properly. The focus of registrar surveillance audits is to ensure continued compliance with the ISO 9001:2008 standard. Auditors look for evidence that the QMS is being maintained in its entirety and improved and corrected as needed.

Organizations that are continually maintaining and improving their QMS are sure to be in "good shape" during surveillance audits.

### Surveillance audits include:

- Review of complaints

- ➤ Findings from internal audits
- ➤ Verification of corrective action
- ➤ Assessment of any changes that have taken place in the QMS

Expect most clauses of the QMS, document control, and record keeping to be reviewed on each visit. Not all registrars will review every clause of the ISO 9001:2008 standard on every visit. If not, they will cover all the clauses over a registration period of three years. In most cases, registrars perform surveillance visits twice a year.

If a major nonconformity is uncovered during a surveillance visit, the auditor will work with you on the required corrective action and conduct an onsite follow-up audit to avoid the necessity of withdrawing your registration certificate until corrective action has taken place.

Surveillance audits supplement the two activities that your organization conducts to ensure continued conformance to ISO 9001:2008 requirements: the Internal Audit (sub-clause 8.2.2) and Management Review (sub-clause 5.6).

Across all levels and all functions, the following checklist displays a checklist of key areas, questions, and tasks that your organization should consider when getting ready.

This checklist should use primarily open-ended questions and be developed by the internal audit team before each internal audit; it should be based on current process performance.

| Area of Preparation ✔ | Questions/ Tasks |
|---|---|
| **Quality Manual** | ❑ Is it complete?<br>❑ Does it contain all elements that you want to be registered? Are there other standards in addition to the ISO 9001 standard? |
| **Application for Registration** | ❑ Have you selected your registrar?<br>❑ Have you completed the application for registration and assessment?<br>❑ Does this company provide the long-term relationship you are seeking? |
| **Internal Audits** | ❑ Have you reviewed all recent (last two years) internal audits to ensure that all items are closed?<br>❑ Were there any systems issues that should be re-reviewed at this time? |
| **Audit Agenda** | ❑ Has this been finalized? Are all areas that you consider important scheduled to be assessed (so you get the most out of the assessment)? |
| **Procedures** | ❑ Are all standard operating procedures current with the quality manual policies and requirements?<br>❑ Do procedures in all areas correspond to the current revision status? Is the control of procedure revisions well understood by all personnel (and adhered to)? |

*Continued on next page*

| | |
|---|---|
| **Training** | ❑ Do all employees understand the quality policy and objectives for quality? Do they understand the quality manual and systems that affect them? |
| | ❑ Are all records for this training current? |
| | ❑ Have all senior managers and line personnel from areas to be visited been briefed on the assessment? |
| **Procedural Documentation** | ❑ Is there documentation in all areas of the assessment? |
| | ❑ Are the records complete and up to date? Do they reflect the procedural requirements that created them? |
| **Assessment Documentation** | ❑ Has an assessment coordinator been appointed? |
| | ❑ Will someone be available to take complete notes during the assessment? |
| **Daily Briefings** | ❑ Have arrangements been made for daily debriefings of each day's assessment activities? (*This is an opportunity to take immediate corrective action on minor observations.*) |

Adapted from a paper presented by Dr. Steve Wirkus, Advanced Cardiovascular Systems, Inc., Temecula, CA, at the ASQ 49th Annual Quality Congress. (Reprinted with permission of the American Society for Quality.)

## Lessons Learned in Implementing ISO 9001:2008

- ✦ Obtain support from upper management

- ✦ Manage ISO 9000 as a company-wide project

- ✦ Set individual management goals and evaluate them periodically

- ✦ Budget resources in advance

- ✦ Be selective in choosing your registrar

- ✦ Adopt ISO 9000 by using a cross-functional team approach (not just a quality assurance department task group)

- ✦ Research and benchmark a company that has been successfully registered

- ✦ Flowchart all activities, not just production activities

- ✦ Develop a training matrix

- ✦ Take time to celebrate along the way

Experience of Haworth, Inc., Holland, MI, as related by William J. Vance, Quality Systems Manager

### More Lessons Learned

- ✦ Communicate early and often with everyone

- ✦ Develop a rapport with your registrar

- ✦ Pay attention to the details

- ✦ Develop well-written procedures. Make sure people are trained on writing effective specifications

- ✦ Continually look for ways to simplify and improve your work

## Summary of Content of ISO 9001:2008

This international standard is organized into nine primary sections.

| 0 | Introduction, relationship to ISO 9004 and ISO 14001, process approach, goal | |
| 1 | Scope | |
| 2 | Normative References | |
| 3 | Terms and Definitions | |
| 4 | Quality Management System | 86 |
| 5 | Management Responsibility | 88 |
| 6 | Resource Management | 89 |
| 7 | Product Realization | 90 |
| 8 | Measurement, Analysis, and Improvement | 92 |

The QMS requirements sections of ISO 9001:2008 are contained in sections 4 through 8. These are explained in greater detail in chapters 4 through 8 of this pocket guide. Following is an overview of these five sections.

# ISO 9001:2008...a brief overview

## QMS Requirements (Section 4)

Under this clause, emphasis is placed on the need for a QMS with a focus on continual improvement.

The necessary steps to implement a QMS are given:

a) Determine the processes needed for the QMS and their application throughout the organization

b) Determine sequence and interactions of these processes, to show how they work together to produce products and provide services

c) Determine criteria and methods needed to ensure both the operation and control of these processes are effective and efficient

d) Ensure the availability of resources and information necessary to support the operation and monitoring of these processes

e) Monitor, measure (quality of linked outputs) and analyze these processes

f) Implement action necessary to achieve planned results and continual improvement of processes

Any outsourced processes affecting product conformity to requirements must be identified and controlled.

QMS documentation must detail procedures that the organization uses to ensure effective operation and control of it processes. This documentation must be monitored to ensure that the correct people have the most recent revisions. Furthermore, document control must be described in a documented procedure. This is first of six requirements that must be covered in a documented procedure.

Records are established and controlled to provide evidence of an effectively implemented and maintained quality system. The control of records must be described in a documented procedure. This is the second of six requirements that must be covered in a documented procedure.

A quality manual is required, covering the scope of the QMS. The organization must specify and justify any exclusions of the ISO 9001:2008 requirements in the quality manual. The quality manual must also describe the sequence and interaction of the processes included in the QMS. Finally, the quality manual must contain or make reference to the procedures required in this Standard. Six items must be covered in one or more procedures: one procedure may cover more than one required item.

Documentation is provided by the organization to ensure that a task is performed completely and accurately. Records are a special type of documentation that provide a history of what was used, happened, recorded on a form, ordered, received, etc.

### Management Responsibility (Section 5)

The Standard emphasizes top management's commitment to quality. This section reinforces the direct involvement of top management with customer requirements.

Top management establishes its policy for quality. Particular attention is given to *a commitment to meeting requirements and to continual improvement, and a framework for establishing and reviewing quality (business) objectives.*

In this section, the requirement is stressed for *quality*

*objectives, at relevant functions and levels within the organi-zation.* These quality objectives must be understood, measurable, and consistent with the quality policy.

Management ensures that management system change is included in planning. The responsibilities and authorities, and their interrelation, are defined within the organization by top management. Only by knowing who is responsible and accountable for a task or a job can one be certain that it will get done.

Top management appoints a member of the organization's management to oversee this process. The manager's clear authority includes promoting awareness of customer requirements throughout the organization. The management representative normally helps the rest of top management periodically review the business management system for performance suitability, adequacy, and effectiveness.

Management ensures that communication takes place between all levels and functions regarding the business management system processes, and their effectiveness and efficiency.

### Resource Management (Section 6)

This clause details the requirement for an organization to determine and enable a culture that provides resources in a timely manner to ensure the implementation of business management system process improvements that directly address customer satisfaction.

The scope of this section also includes training resources and ensuring that training is effective. The emphasis is on ensuring competence of personnel performing work that affects conformity to product requirements. This conformity can be affected either directly or indirectly by competent personnel.

The organization must also identify, provide, and maintain the facilities needed to achieve the conformity of product.

The organization must identify and manage buildings, equipment, infrastructure, and human and physical factors of the work environment that are needed to achieve both product conformance and process capability.

### Product Realization (Section 7)

Product Realization is defined as "that sequence of processes and sub processes required to achieve the product." This is how your product is designed, validated, produced, tested, handled, shipped, etc. Your customer may also have specific requirements (including guidance documents) for you to follow to carry out product realization.

Emphasis is placed on how the organization understands, communicates, implements, and meets customer requirements.

The organization must design and develop their product and processes to achieve product conformity. The product design and development of ISO 9001:2008 requirements can be excluded from your business management system if the organization is not responsible for product design (see information in 1.2 Application). However, the information in this section may be used for manufacturing process design even if the organization is not responsible for product design. Design and development reviews must be *systematic* in ensuring conformance with input requirements. Changes must be verified and validated before implementation.

A purchasing process ensures that you use conforming raw materials and other process inputs to perform your work. Your organization must evaluate, approve, and keep records on selected suppliers.

You must have processes that are controlled. A process that is under control is predictable. Methods of control may include work instructions, suitable equipment, availability and use of monitoring and measuring equipment, implementation of monitoring and measurement, and implementation of product release, delivery, and post-delivery activities. Processes where the end result cannot be checked or measured must be validated. A validation guarantees the process does what it is supposed to do. Typically, process validation criteria are based on existing process standards, such as Society of Automotive Engineers (SAE), ASTM International (ASTM), etc.

You must be able to identify one product from another. You may also be required to track your products by a unique identification method. This would allow you to trace back to the material suppliers or to trace forward to where the product was ultimately delivered. It is also a requirement to identify the product status according to monitoring and measurement. Typically, product status uses a material tagging scheme or bar coding.

Customer property that is used by you or in your care must be identified, verified, protected and or safeguarded. Customer property may include intellectual property and personal data.

To preserve the conformity of product, your final product and all constituent parts must be identified, handled, packaged, stored, and protected while being handled. This includes delivery to the intended destination.

You must ensure valid results from your monitoring and measuring equipment. Controls would include calibration, adjustment, readjustment, protection, and other control issues.

Typically, the organization uses measurement system analysis to help understand measurement system variation and its impact on measurement equipment capability.

### Measurement, Analysis, and Improvement (Section 8)

Measurement and monitoring activities needed to assure conformity and achieve improvement must be defined, planned, and implemented. Measuring and monitoring allows the organization to manage by fact—not by guess or opinion.

The organization must monitor information relating to customer perception as to whether the organization has fulfilled customer requirements.

Internal auditing must be done at regular intervals to determine if the system is working as planned. Audits are checks on the business management system, not on individuals. An audit of your area is an opportunity for management to find ways to improve your process by supporting improvements. Always answer an auditor's questions openly and honestly. Internal auditing must be described in a documented procedure. This is the third of six requirements that must be covered in a documented procedure.

The control of nonconforming product must be described in a documented procedure. The organization must protect the customer and containment any product that is known to be non-conforming. Once the non-conforming product is corrected, it must be reverified to ensure its product conformity. Any situation where non-conforming products might reach your customer should trigger an immediate corrective action.

This clause also highlights the analysis of applicable data as one means of determining where QMS improvements can be made.

The organization must plan and manage the processes for the continual improvement of the business management system. The organization must use the quality policy, objectives, management reviews, customer satisfaction data, internal audit results, analysis of data, corrective and preventive action, and management review to facilitate continual improvement.

Corrective action must be described in a documented procedure. Corrective action includes correcting nonconformity and preventing it from happening again. This is the fifth of six requirements that must be covered in a documented procedure.

Preventive action must also be described in a documented procedure. Preventive action keeps the undesired result from ever occurring. This is the sixth of six requirements that must be covered in a documented procedure.

The emphasis in your organization's QMS should be prevention and/or prediction of nonconforming output.

# Part
# TWO

# QUALITY
# MANAGEMENT SYSTEM

4.1 General Requirements ............................. 96

4.2.1 General............................................ 97

4.2.2 Quality Manual .................................. 98

4.2.3 Control of Documents ......................... 98

4.2.4 Provide for Control of Records.............. 99

## Why do it?

To make certain that your QMS provides products and services that meet your customers' needs and will continually improve your ability to add value consistently in the future.

### What is it?

A means to demonstrate, through processes and documented procedures, that:

- Quality plans are implemented and efficient
- The overall system is in effective use
- The QMS is continually improving

 ### How do I do it?

#### Establish existing company practices (4.1.a and b) by using:

- Process maps
- Flow charts
- Procedures (written and unwritten)
- Work/job instructions

Ensure these processes are under controlled (predictable) conditions that meet desired outcomes (effective) (4.1.c).

Evaluate resources and information are present and needed (4.1.d).

- Personnel
- Facilities
- Equipment
- Specifications and acceptance standards
- Records

Monitor, measure, and (where applicable) analyze these processes (4.1.e).

Implement the quality system (4.1.f).

- Review processes
- Plan needed resources/time frames
- Update procedures and instrumentation
- Seek ways to achieve continual improvement
- Identify measurement requirements
- Clarify acceptance standards
- Maintain quality records
- Control outsourced processes
- Ensure all requirements of ISO 9001:2008 are being met

### What processes are applicable to 4.1?

- Business planning (QMS Planning)
- Management review
- All processes of your QMS are described as a system of processes

### How do I know it's working (measurables)?

Improvements in key performance indicators

> These indicators must be objective, measurable, targeted, and time bounded.

---

## Documentation Requirements

- Plan the structure of the documentation (4.2.1)

### Prepare a quality manual (4.2.2)

Items that may be included
*italicized items* **must** *be included:*

- *Scope of the QMS*
- *Exclusions, and why they have been made*
- *Sequence and interaction between QMS processes*
- *Procedures required by ISO 9001:2008 or references to these procedures*
- Quality policy
- Organizational chart
- Quality assurance organization
- Statement of authority and responsibility
- Distribution list of controlled copies
- Forms index
- Job instructions
- Records
- Specifications
- Statutory and regulatory requirements

### Control of documents (4.2.3)

- List all documents where a procedure is required
- Develop a plan for control of all documents,

including review, updating, re-approval, issuing and distribution (4.2.4 requirements apply)

- Before being issued, verify that documents are adequate, legible, and easily identified
- May be in any form or type of media
- Identify the current revision status of all documents
- As necessary, reapprove documents
- Ensure accessibility to documents at the work/job location
- Establish control over documents that become obsolete, including removal and controlled retention
- Identify and control documents originating from outside the organization
- A master list (or equivalent control) could be used to show current revision status of all documents and be readily available to avoid the use of the wrong documents
- Current documents are to be in use where needed

## Provide for control of records (4.2.4)

- Controls must demonstrate that requirements are being met and are effective
- Procedures for identification, storage, retrieval, protection, retention time, and disposal of records must be established
- Records must be readable and easily identified
- Records retention requirements of customers and regulatory agencies must be met

### Examples of documents

- Processes: COP, support, management, etc.
- Documents necessary to maintain the business management system
- Procedures for data approval and control
- Master list of documents and records (data sheets)
- Schedule for review of documents and records
- Procedures to control quality records
- Index of records
- Retention and disposal schedule for records
- Engineering and material drawings
- Specifications (products and processes)
- Test procedures and inspection instructions
- Operation sheets
- Quality assurance procedures
- Quality records, and documents defined as quality records
- Quality plans
- Quality manual
- Operating procedures
- Work/job instructions

### Examples of records

- ◆◆ Management review (5.6.1)

- ◆◆ Training, education, skills, and experience (6.2.2)

- ◆◆ Processes and products compliance (7.1)

- ◆◆ Contract review and amendments (7.2.2)

- ◆◆ Design records (7.3.2, 7.3.4, 7.3.5, 7.3.6, and 7.3.7)

- ◆◆ Purchasing records (7.4.1)

- ◆◆ Verification of controls (7.5.1)

- ◆◆ Validation results (7.5.2)

- ◆◆ Product records (7.5.3)

- ◆◆ Traceability (7.5.3)

- ◆◆ Customer property (7.5.4)

- ◆◆ Calibration records (7.6)

- ◆◆ Internal audit plans and results (8.2.2)

- ◆◆ Product release authorization (8.2.4)

- ◆◆ Nonconforming product (8.3)

- ◆◆ Corrective action identification, disposition, and effectiveness (8.5.2)

- ◆◆ Preventive action identification, disposition and effectiveness (8.5.3)

### What processes support

→ Document control

→ Control of records

### How do I know it's working (measurables)?

→ Timely document review and release

→ Number of uncontrolled documents found during audits

→ Accuracy of documents

→ Document accuracy and accessibility

 **Pitfalls**

→ The quality system is not viewed as a process

→ The quality system is separate and running parallel to the business system

→ Interaction between QMS processes is not understood

→ The quality system is not adequately documented

→ The quality system is over-documented without consistent implementation

→ The quality manual is not complete, is obsolete or not practical

→ Inadequate control of standards and specifications (i.e., timing, distribution, updating)

→ Unauthorized changes to documents

→ Inspection procedures are insufficient

- Testing methods are incorrect
- No records exist to verify the effectiveness of approved process controls, or retention policy is not followed
- Records and documents are not readily available
- Records and documents are not legible

| Factors to Consider in the Control of Quality Records | |
|---|---|
| **Identification** | Designation of individual records |
| **Collection** | Responsibility for record collection |
| **Indexing** | An indexing structure providing an access trail |
| **Access** | Provision for ready access of quality records for those using them |
| **Filing** | Filing quality records where access is easy, during the high review part of the record's life |
| **Storage** | Less accessible bulk storage during archival part of record life |
| **Maintenance** | Records are to demonstrate conformance to specified requirements and effective quality system operation. Supplier quality records may be an element of such data |
| **Legibility** | Readable under normal operating conditions |
| **Retention times** | Established, recorded, and administered |
| **Form of records** | Hard copy, electronic, or other media |

Sample Format
(To use in writing either a section of a quality
manual or describing a quality system procedure.)

| Organization | | Title/Subject | | Number | |
|---|---|---|---|---|---|
| Unit Issuing | Approved by | Date | | Revision | Page |

**Policy/Policy Reference**
State the governing requirement.

**Purpose and Scope**
State why the document or procedure is used or what it
accomplishes, the area it covers, and any exclusions
or exceptions.

**Responsibility**
Identify the organizational unit or units responsible
for implementing the document that will achieve the
purpose.

**Action/Method** to Achieve System Element Requirement.
List the details, step by step, of what needs to be
done. Use references if appropriate. Put the list of
items in a logical sequence. Mention any exceptions or
specific areas of attention.

**Documentation/References**
Identify which referenced documents or forms are
associated with using the document, or what data have
to be recorded. Use examples if appropriate.

**Records**
Identify which records are generated as a result of
using the document, where these records are retained,
and the length of time they are retained.

Note 1: The structure and order of the items you choose to use in
your documentation format should be based on your own
organizational needs.

Note 2: Approval and revision status should be identified on the
documentation.

Adapted from ANSI/ISO/ASQ Q10013, p. 7.
Reprinted with permission of the American Society for Quality.

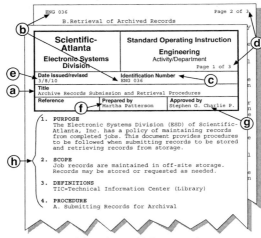

ENG 036                                            Page 2 of 3

B. Retrieval of Archived Records

| **Scientific-Atlanta** Electronic Systems Division | **Standard Operating Instruction** **Engineering** Activity/Department Page 1 of 3 |
|---|---|
| Date issued/revised 3/8/10 | Identification Number ENG 036 |
| Title Archive Records Submission and Retrieval Procedures | |
| Reference | Prepared by Martha Patterson | Approved by Stephen G. Charlie P. |

1. **PURPOSE**
   The Electronic Systems Division (ESD) of Scientific-Atlanta, Inc. has a policy of maintaining records from completed jobs. This document provides procedures to be followed when submitting records to be stored and retrieving records from storage.

2. **SCOPE**
   Job records are maintained in off-site storage. Records may be stored or requested as needed.

3. **DEFINITIONS**
   TIC=Technical Information Center (Library)

4. **PROCEDURE**
   A. Submitting Records for Archival

Information provided courtesy of
Sam Tolbert, Scientific Atlanta

**A "controlled document" will have:**

(a) **Title**

(b) **Document number** (a unique identifier)

(c) **Revision indicator** (e.g., Rev. A, -001, [blank]: in this case it is blank)

(d) **Page number** (e.g., Page 1 of 3, Page 1.2, 1-2.3)

(e) **Date issued/revised** (e.g., April 6, 2010, 4/6/10)

(f) **Prepared by/issued by** (name, position, and/or department)

(g) **Approval** (the approving authority by signature and perhaps also position title)

(h) **Document content**

Example of a Quality Document

| INSPECTION INSTRUCTION NO. ___ | ☐ Incoming | ☐ In-Process | ☐ Final | Page ___ of ___ |

Part No. ___
Part Name ___
Sampling Reference ___
Prepared by ___

**Part Sketch**

Supplier Name ___
Laboratory Required ___ No. ___
Equipment No. ___ Line No. ___
Revisions ___
Approved by ___ Date ___

| Operation No. | Char. No. | C/C* | Characteristic Description | Limits | Sample Size | Inspection Equipment/Method | Equipment Numbers |
|---|---|---|---|---|---|---|---|
| | | | | | | | |
| | | | | | | | |
| | | | | | | | |
| | | | | | | | |
| | | | | | | | |
| | | | | | | | |
| | | | | | | | |
| | | | | | | | |
| | | | | | | | |
| | | | | | | | |
| | | | | | | | |
| | | | | | | | |
| | | | | | | | |

*Characteristic Classification    C = Critical    M = Major    N = Minor    I = Incidental

Provided by Frank Caplan, Quality Sciences
Consultants, Inc. Developed as an exhibit for
*The Quality System: A Sourcebook for Managers and Engineers,*
by Frank Caplan, Chilton Book Co.

The Memory Jogger™ 9001:2008 | ©2009 GOAL/QPC

# Chapter
## FIVE

# Management Responsibility

5.1 Ensure Management Commitment............ 110

5.2 Focus on the Customer ............................. 110

5.3 Establish a Quality Policy ........................ 110

5.4 Define Quality Objectives/Planning .......... 111

5.5 Demonstrate Responsibility, Authority and Communication ......................................... 112

5.6 Management Review .................................. 113

## Why do it?

To ensure that top management takes a direct leadership role in defining, implementing, administering, and improving the business management system, with the goal of meeting all customer requirements.

### What is it?

A participative commitment of top management's responsibilities in establishing, reviewing, and providing resources to support the company's business process improvement. Top management is defined as a "person or group of people who directs and controls an organization at the highest level" according to ISO 9000:2005.

 ### How do I do it?

### Ensure management commitment (5.1)

- ➡ Communicate importance of meeting customer, statutory, and regulatory requirements
- ➡ Establish a quality policy and quality objectives
- ➡ Develop and implement a business plan
- ➡ Conduct management reviews
- ➡ Provide all needed resources

### Focus on the customer (5.2)

- ➡ Demonstrate that customer, statutory, and regulatory requirements are defined, translated into requirements, and are being met

### Establish a quality policy (5.3)

- ➡ Assign responsibility to a cross-process and functional team to develop the quality policy. It should include:

  ▶ The organization's quality objectives

---

▶ Management's commitment to meet requirements and to continually improve

▶ Relevance to organizational goals

▶ Expectations and needs of customers

➡ Ask for cross-functional input to ensure direct contribution, accountability, and "ownership" of the quality policy

➡ Develop comprehensive objectives that align with the business plan

➡ Verify that the policy is communicated to and understood by everyone in the organization. You can help by:

▶ Conducting an orientation for new employees

▶ Displaying copies of the policy

▶ Conducting departmental meetings/discussions

▶ Reinforcing and following up on improvement ideas of the policy

▶ Verifying that awareness and understanding are uniform

➡ Periodically evaluate the quality policy for suitability

### Define quality objectives (5.4)

➡ Establish quality objectives and measures throughout the organization. Measurable objectives are set by top management to be used as a leadership tool that provides a focused direction that fits within the framework of the quality policy

The intent of setting objectives is to show results from a continually improving organization

- ✸✸ Ensure that all objectives can be measured, address customer expectations, and can be met in a defined time period
- ✸✸ Commit to continual improvement of both product and processes
- ✸✸ Plan to meet product quality requirements
- ✸✸ Plan actions to meet and document results
- ✸✸ Identify what ISO 9001:2008 requirements can be excluded
- ✸✸ Plan for the provision of the resources needed for implementation of a QMS
- ✸✸ Ensure changes take place in a controlled manner

### Demonstrate that your QMS is well administered (5.5)

- ✸✸ Define areas of responsibility and authority
  - ❱ Use organizational charts, as necessary
  - ❱ Include job descriptions, roles, and responsibilities for everyone in the organization that supports the scope
  - ❱ Communicate these roles and responsibilities to everyone affected
- ✸✸ Appoint a management representative who:
  - ❱ Is a member of the organization's management team
  - ❱ Ensures that the quality system is established and implemented

- Reports on the performance of the quality system
- Ensures that customer needs are well known
- Interfaces with outside parties on product or service issues

♦ Provide for internal communication
- Demonstrate that the value of the QMS and its effectiveness are communicated to all levels and functions (5.5.3)

### Provide for management review of the quality system (5.6)

♦ Ensure suitability and effectiveness in meeting policy and objectives (5.6.1)

♦ Determine if quality systems changes, such as policy and objectives, are needed, for continual improvement
- Include performance trends and implications (5.6.1.1)

♦ Review current performance and look for improvement opportunities by (5.6.2):
- Assessing audit results
- Reviewing customer feedback
- Observing performance of the process and conformance of the product
- Assessing preventive and corrective actions
- Reviewing follow-up actions from previous product or process reviews
- Considering ways to improve the QMS

- ➔ Identify actions to (5.6.3):
  - ▶ Improve the QMS
  - ▶ Improve the product and processes
  - ▶ Provide resources (people, facilities, equipment)
- ➔ Maintain review records (5.6.3)

## *Guidance in Preparing the Quality Policy*

- ➔ Make it understandable
- ➔ Make it ambitious, yet achievable
- ➔ Relate objectives to performance (including quality goals), fitness for use, safety, and reliability
- ➔ Consider total costs to minimize losses
- ➔ Establish quality objectives at appropriate levels of management
- ➔ Provide sufficient resources to reach the objectives
- ➔ Determine and provide the necessary training that will result in competent employees
- ➔ Control all activities that affect quality
- ➔ Emphasize prevention, and variation and waste reduction

### Guidance in Preparing Documents

Ensure clear assignments of individual responsibility, lines of authority, and interrelationship of all personnel whose work affects quality. Special attention should be given to personnel assigned to:

- Initiate preventive action
- Identify and recommend solutions to problems
- Verify implementation of correction
- Control further production and distribution activities until problem is corrected
- Make a record of resource requirements and in-house verification activities

#### Examples of documents

- Documents necessary to maintain the QMS
- Quality plans (manufacturing control plans, routings, job sheets, etc.)
- Operating procedures
- Work/job instructions
- Procedures to control documents
- Management review procedures
- Inspection procedures and instructions

### Examples of records

- Corrective action taken
- Evidence of conformance of operation of the QMS
- Dissemination of quality policy, for understanding, implementation, and maintenance
- Management review of records of results
- Quality records specified on documentation procedures
- Results of document and data reviews
- Distribution lists

### What processes are applicable?

- Business planning
- Product and process planning
- Management review
- Customer satisfaction
- Continual improvement
- Resource management
- Communication

### How do I know it's working (measurables)?

- Customer satisfaction results
- Communication that takes place is timely and effective

- ➔ Objectives are accomplished
- ➔ Continual improvement trends
- ➔ Management reviews are conducted on time
- ➔ Outputs from management review are accomplished

 **Pitfalls**

### Management Commitment and Responsibility

- ➔ Managers have no written statement of their responsibilities, authority, and accountability
- ➔ Managers are not directly involved with the business system
- ➔ Managers delegate everything to the quality function
- ➔ Managing two separate systems (quality and business management)
- ➔ Managers are not implementing their responsibility and authority
- ➔ Where an organization chart is used, there is no back-up information on the systems or interfaces
- ➔ Interfaces and relationships between personnel and departments do not exist or are not defined
- ➔ There is no quality plan for a specific product/project that requires a deviation/addition to the normal procedures contained in the quality manual

‿

•• Too much design is taking place without production involvement, and this is causing production to deviate from an impossible-to-achieve specification

### *Quality Policy*

•• No policy statement exists

•• A policy statement is written, but not understood or implemented at all levels, particularly on the shop floor

•• Objectives are not clearly defined or missing

•• No real control system exists

•• No accountability

•• No single individual has been assigned responsibility

•• There is no disciplined recall system for obsolete or modified documents

•• Work/job instructions are not at the place of work

•• There are unauthorized changes in documents

•• Changes are not made to all documents that are issued, or there are penciled changes

•• Changes are not verified with the function that issued or the document

•• Personnel lack competence to do their job

### *Management Representative*

- ◆◆ The management representative has inadequately defined responsibility and authority

- ◆◆ The management representative is not implementing his/her defined responsibilities and authority

- ◆◆ The management representative is a consultant and not a member of the organization

- ◆◆ The management representative has no authority

### *Management Review*

- ◆◆ No review system exists

- ◆◆ Corrective action on internal audit results has not been carried out

- ◆◆ Management review is thought of as an event not a process

Partial Example of a Format of a
Quality Plan for a Processed Material

| Part | Process Flowchart | Process Stage | Work Instruction Number | Quality characteristic to be controlled (Process condition to be checked) | Process Control | | | | Inspection | |
|---|---|---|---|---|---|---|---|---|---|---|
| | | | | | Instruction for Process Control Number | Control Method | Responsible Function | Verification/Instruction | Parameters | Procedure Number |
| Part A | ● | Pre-heating | WI-123 | Temperature | IPC-22 | Check Sheet Ref. No. 1 | Work-station A | VI-29 | | |
| | ● | Forming | WI-321 | Temperature, pressure | | Check Sheet Ref. No. 2 | B | | | |
| | ● | Cutting | | Length | | | C | | | |
| | ◇ | | | Measure length | | Control Chart Ref. No. 1 | D | | | |
| | ▷ | | | Yield | | | | | Length | IT-5 |

**Symbol Key:**

● Manufacturing

◇ Inspection and testing

▷ Storage

BSR/ANSI/ISO/ASQ Q10005. Reprinted with permission
of the American Society for Quality.

Quality Plan for Service Calls
(For defining areas of responsibility and authority)

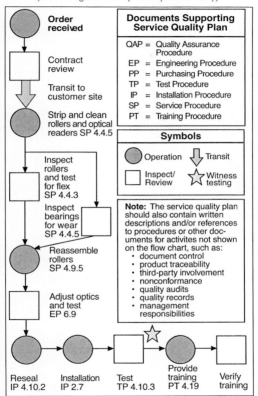

| **Documents Supporting Service Quality Plan** |
| QAP = Quality Assurance Procedure |
| EP = Engineering Procedure |
| PP = Purchasing Procedure |
| TP = Test Procedure |
| IP = Installation Procedure |
| SP = Service Procedure |
| PT = Training Procedure |

Order received

Contract review

Transit to customer site

Strip and clean rollers and optical readers SP 4.4.5

Inspect rollers and test for flex SP 4.4.3

Inspect bearings for wear SP 4.4.5

Reassemble rollers SP 4.9.5

Adjust optics and test EP 6.9

Reseal IP 4.10.2

Installation IP 2.7

Test TP 4.10.3

Provide training PT 4.19

Verify training

**Symbols**

⬤ Operation  ⬇ Transit

☐ Inspect/Review  ☆ Witness testing

**Note:** The service quality plan should also contain written descriptions and/or references to procedures or other documents for activites not shown on the flow chart, such as:
- document control
- product traceability
- third-party involvement
- nonconformance
- quality audits
- quality records
- management responsibilities

BSR/ANSI/ISO/ASQ Q10005. Reprinted with permission of the American Society for Quality.

©2009 GOAL/QPC

The Memory Jogger™ 9001:2008 | ©2009 GOAL/QPC

# Chapter
## SIX

# RESOURCE MANAGEMENT

6.1 Provision of Resources ............................ 124

6.2 Human Resources ................................... 124

6.3 Infrastructure ....................................... 126

6.4 Work environment ................................. 126

### Why do it?

To make certain that adequate physical and human resources are available to meet all requirements of the QMS.

### What is it?

Processes to determine, provide for, and manage all required resources to implement and maintain the QMS, continually improve its effectiveness and enhance customer satisfaction. This includes the people, equipment, and facilities of the business management system.

 *How do I do it?*

## Provision of resources (6.1)

*Identify and provide resource requirements*

Establish and continually improve the effectiveness of the QMS

- ◆▸ Work performance
- ◆▸ Verification activities
- ◆▸ Quality plan requirements
- ◆▸ Satisfy customers' requirements

## Human resources (6.2)

*Identify training needs*

- ◆▸ List all job functions, including roles and responsibilities, and accountability
- ◆▸ Establish training/competence requirements for each function, i.e., core and developmental skills
- ◆▸ Include the requirements in each job description
- ◆▸ Evaluate training effectiveness

### Establish competence of personnel at all levels, whose work affects quality, including (6.2.2a)

- ◆▸ Education and training (initial, additional)
- ◆▸ Capability to perform work required

- Previous experience
- Physical characteristics and limitations
- Medical records
- Awards, rewards, promotions
- Output of work performed
- Employee development for both personal and organizational needs

### Develop and execute a training plan that includes (6.2.2b, c d and e)

- Required training
- Optional additional training
- Cross-training
- Qualifications of trainers
- Special training (safety, SPC)
- Process knowledge requirements: methods, equipment
- Product knowledge requirements: specifications; workmanship standards
- Extent of trainee's knowledge and skills
- Periodic evaluation of effectiveness and competence
- Confirmation of the effectiveness of training
- Maintain records, either external or internal
- Ensure personnel are aware of their importance in helping the organization achieve its objectives

*Infrastructure: Identify the necessary physical resources to produce your product or provide your service (6.3)*

↔ Buildings, floorspace and utilities

↔ Equipment needed for processing, including hardware and software

↔ Services providing transportation, communication, equipment maintenance, etc.

*Work environment (6.4)*

↔ Establish and maintain a work environment that makes meeting product requirements possible

↔ Devise means of minimizing risks to employees, especially those involved in product design and manufacturing

↔ Emphasize personnel safety regardless of work assignment

### Examples of documents

↔ Quality system training needs

↔ Training procedures for each function

↔ Job descriptions

↔ Training modules

↔ List of qualified trainers

↔ Plant layout including equipment

↔ Safety rules

- ◆◆ Preventive maintenance schedules
- ◆◆ Hazardous materials handling procedures

### Examples of records

- ◆◆ Personnel skills, education, experience, and training
- ◆◆ Training plans for operators
- ◆◆ Required training certifications
- ◆◆ Safety records
- ◆◆ External training records such as certificates, diplomas, etc.

### Examples of processes that might be applicable

- ◆◆ Training
- ◆◆ Resource planning
- ◆◆ Communication
- ◆◆ Preventive maintenance
- ◆◆ Work environment
- ◆◆ Risk management

### How do I know it's working? (measurement examples)

- ◆◆ Training is completed on time

- Personnel are competent (look at output)
- Absenteeism
- Safety incidents
- Maintenance is completed on-time
- Personnel have certifications, licenses, etc.

#  Pitfalls

- A lack of adequate resources
- A lack of trained/competent personnel (the organization defines required training, but does not follow its own rules)
- No relationships/interfaces, particularly with feedback from installation and servicing
- Agency personnel are not receiving adequate training
- No records exist or records are inadequate
- Inadequate documentation of procedures
- A lack of appropriate education, training or experience
- Training needs are not assessed or the training plan is inadequate
- The environment does not encourage innovation and improvement
- Personnel don't understand how they contribute to the achievement of the organization's objectives
- Developmental training may not be available

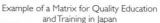

Example of a Matrix for Quality Education
and Training in Japan

| People / Topic | Top Management | Middle Mgmt./Staff | Engineers | Supervisors | Function & Administration | General Workers |
|---|---|---|---|---|---|---|
| TQM Concepts | ○ | ○ | ○ | ○ | △/◎ | ○ |
| TQM Techniques | ○ | ○ | ◎ | ◎ | | ○ |
| Statistical Methods | ○ | ○ | ◎ | ○ | ○ | ○ |
| Quality Assurance | △ | ○ | ◎ | ○ | △ | △ |
| Product Development | △ | △ | ◎ | | △/○ | |
| Role in TQM | ◎ | ◎ | ◎ | ◎ | ◎ | ◎ |
| QC Circle | △ | ○ | △ | ◎ | △ | ○/◎ |
| New Product Introduction | ○ | △ | ◎ | ○ | | |
| Hoshin Planning | ◎ | ○ | △ | | △ | |
| Company Production System | | | ○ | ◎ | | ○ |

Educated to:  △ = Understand    ○ = Use    ◎ = Master

Excerpt from GOAL/QPC Research Committee Research Report,
"Total Quality Control Education in Japan," p. 9

## Partial Example of a Knowledge, Skills, and Abilities Matrix

**Legend (Dept #/name: 570 — Quality Systems):**
- (R) Required
- (D) Desirable
- (na) Not Applicable
- (94) Year Scheduled
- (C) Completed

| | | Director — Manos, K | Quality Manager — Vance, B | Booker, B | Sr. Quality Engnr — McMurray, D | Smith, G |
|---|---|---|---|---|---|---|
| **Quality** | | | | | | |
| Process Activity Analysis | 4 hrs. | na | D | C | D | D |
| Project Mgmt. | 24 hrs. | D | D | 95 | C | C |
| GDT Overview (Managers course) | 16 hrs. | na | D | C | C | 95 |
| GDT Specifier | 40 hrs. | na | D | C | D | D |
| GDT Interpreter | 24 hrs. | na | R | D | D | C |
| Reliability in Prod. Design/Test | 24 hrs. | na | R | R | R | C |
| QFD | 2 hrs. | na | R | R | R | C |
| FMEA | 4 hrs. | na | R | 94 | R | C |
| DOE | 32 hrs. | na | R | 96 | R | C |
| Chart Interpretation | 4 hrs. | na | R | C | R | C |
| Pre-Control | 2 hrs. | na | R | C | R | C |
| Basic SPC Charting | 10 hrs. | na | R | C | R | C |
| Process Capability /Dist. Analysis | 24 hrs. | na | R | C | R | C |
| Mfg. Planning Process Control | 2 hrs. | na | R | C | R | C |
| **Members Who Supervise/Manage Others** | | | | | | |
| Managing Personal Growth (D) | 13 hrs. | R | 94 | R | na | C |
| Managing Diversity (D) | 9 hrs. | R | 94 | 95 | 94 | C |
| Selection Interviewing (D) | 12 hrs. | R | 94 | 95 | 95 | C |
| Quality Improvement Fac. (D) | 4 hrs. | R | 94 | 95 | 96 | C |
| Performance Appraisal Trng. (R) | 6 hrs. | R | 95 | C | 95 | C |
| Haworth Policies (R) | | R | 94 | 95 | 94 | C |
| Delegation (R) | 8 hrs. | R | 94 | 94 | 94 | C |
| Conflict Resolution (R) | 16 hrs. | R | 94 | 94 | 94 | C |
| Managing Change (R) | 16 hrs. | R | 94 | 94 | 94 | C |
| Interpersonal Mgmt. Skills (R) | 12 hrs. | R | 94 | C | C | C |
| Sexual Harassment (R) | 4 hrs. | R | 94 | C | C | C |
| Affirmative Action/EEO (R) | 4 hrs. | R | 94 | C | C | C |
| **All Members** | | | | | | |
| Sexual Harrassment (nonmgmt.) (D) | 4 hrs. | na | C | na | D | na |
| JIT (R) | 12 hrs. | R | 94 | C | R | C |
| IDEAS Suggestion System (R) | 2 hrs. | R | 94 | C | C | C |
| 4-Step Problem Solving (R) | 12 hrs. | R | 94 | C | 94 | C |
| Hazard Comm/Right to Know (R) | 1 hr. | R | C | C | C | C |
| Recall Orientation (R) | 7.5 hrs. | R | 94 | C | C | C |
| First Day Orientation (R) | 6.5 hrs. | R | C | C | C | C |

Information provided courtesy of
William J. Vance, Haworth, Inc., Holland, MI

# Chapter
## SEVEN

# PRODUCT REALIZATION

| 7.1 | Planning of Product Realization | 133 |
|---|---|---|
| 7.2 | Customer-Related Processes | 138 |
| | 7.2.1 Determination of Requirements Related to the Product | |
| | 7.2.2 Review of Requirements Related to the Product | |
| | 7.2.3 Customer Communication | |
| 7.3 | Design and Development | 143 |
| | 7.3.1 Planning | |
| | 7.3.2 Inputs | |
| | 7.3.3 Outputs | |
| | 7.3.4 Review | |
| | 7.3.5 Verification | |

    7.3.6 Validation

    7.3.7 Control of Changes

7.4 Purchasing......................................151

    7.4.1 Process

    7.4.2 Information

    7.4.3 Verification of Purchased Product

7.5 Production and Service Provisions ..........158

    7.5.1 Control

    7.5.2 Validation of Processes

    7.5.3 Identification and Traceability

    7.5.4 Customer Property

    7.5.5 Preservation of Product

7.6 Control of Monitoring and Measuring
    Equipment......................................181

### What's changed from ISO 9001:2000?

- ➼ 7.1.c  Addition of measurement

- ➼ 7.1  Changed "provided in a form that enables" to "in a form suitable"

- ➼ 7.2.1  Changed "related" to "applicable," "determined" to "considered necessary," Addition of a note about post-delivery activities

- ➼ 7.3.1  Addition of a note

- ➼ 7.3.3  Deleted the word "for" in bullet b and added a note

- ↔ 7.3.7  Merged paragraphs 1 and 2

- ↔ 7.5.1  Changed word "devices" to "equipment"; added the word "product" in bullet f

- ↔ 7.5.2  Changed wording "this includes any process where" to "and as a consequence"

- ↔ 7.5.4  Reworded sentence about reporting problems with customer property to the customer; added "and personal data" to the note

- ↔ 7.5.5  Changed "This preservation..." to "As applicable, preservation..."

- ↔ 7.6  Added "or both" to bullet a; reworded bullet c; rearranged sentences; changed "NOTE"

# 7.1 Planning of Product Realization

### Why do it?

To make certain that you have plans for all realization processes (planning, design, production, installation, and servicing) to be executed under controlled conditions to ensure that quality (business) objectives are met.

### What is it?

Evidence of planning for the realization of your production, installation, and servicing processes, as appropriate:

- ↔ Objectives are defined and deployed

- The steps to produce/deliver the product or service are identified and planned

- Equipment is identified with a plan to implement the equipment

- Need for documented instructions are identified, for activities affecting quality

- A suitable working environment is defined with implementation requirements

- Processes are monitored, measured and approved

- Workmanship and acceptance criteria are established

- Plans for verification and validation of activities are prepared

- Necessary records are determined

### How do I do it?

- Some customers refer to this as advanced product quality planning or project management

- Include basic process controls on the quality plan. You may need a more comprehensive quality plan that includes the other critical documents and references to give a more complete understanding of the products and the requirements for that product at the characteristic level

- Identify critical control points such as time, temperature, pressure, etc.

- Define factors affecting control of key processes (production, installation, and service):
    - Identify and inventory all production and support equipment
    - Define work environment controls such as temperature, humidity, cleanliness, etc.
    - Hazardous material control
- Identify the following product requirements:
    - Specifications
    - Workmanship standards
    - Regulatory standards and codes
    - Acceptance criteria
- Review existing monitoring techniques
- Develop control and approval processes
- Develop work/job instructions
- Develop production equipment maintenance processes
- Develop verification processes
- Develop validation procedures
- Establish appropriate record system to provide confidence in conformity

### Examples of documents

→→ Quality plan, which includes operation steps, production equipment, product characteristics, process parameters, sampling frequency and size, measurement equipment, and operational reaction plan

→→ Methods for:

- ▶ Product control
- ▶ Monitoring
- ▶ Containment actions
- ▶ Maintenance
- ▶ Change approval

→→ Reference standards and codes (health, safety, and environment)

→→ Product standards, representative samples, and illustrations, as appropriate

→→ Work/job instructions, i.e., standardized work

### Examples of records

→→ Records to show conformity and nonconformity

→→ Process change approvals

→→ Special process approvals of equipment and personnel

→→ Process monitoring results

→→ Process maintenance

→→ Measurement device requirement and controls

## *Examples of processes that might be applicable*

- Design of product
- Design of process
- Sales/quoting
- Product quality planning and approval

## *Examples of linked processes*

- Manufacturing
- Purchasing
- Material transportation
- Product and process engineering
- Business planning

## *Examples of performance measurements*

- Projects completed on time
- Customer satisfaction and returns
- Inbound and outbound materials delivery times
- Inbound materials overages, shortages, and damaged
- Product rework and scrap
- Supplier performance
- Performance to objectives

## Pitfalls

- There is a lack of demonstrable planning for control of personnel, machines, materials, methods of work, environment, etc.
- No objectives have been set for product or process
- There is inadequate planning for validation and verification
- There are inadequate written work instructions/ procedures in cases where their absence could affect quality
- Unclear customer requirements
- Unclear supplier capability

## 7.2 Customer-Related Processes

7.2.1 Determination of requirements related to the product

7.2.2 Review of requirements related to the product

7.2.3 Customer communication and their representatives

### *Why do it?*

To make certain that you will be able to meet your customers' needs before accepting an order. This would include providing the customer's product, at acceptable levels, as required, in the time frame required, and at the cost specified.

### *What is it?*

Documentation that you understand customer needs, are sure that all the requirements are adequately defined, and that any requirements that differ from those in the contract are reconciled. You should follow a procedure for reviewing requests for quotations, contracts, performance criteria, or accepted orders.

 *How do I do it?*

- Document the customer's requirements

- Complete a feasibility review, i.e., price, timing, quality levels, candidate suppliers, material acceptance criteria

- Establish contract or order review procedures

- Verify the capability to meet requirements

- Internalize customer's requirements and resolve any differences

- Maintain control of customer purchase orders that are written under one contract

- Develop a plan for deployment

- Establish customer purchase order review procedures

- Obtain customer agreements

- Revise/improve procedures

- Evaluate revisions

## *Examples of documents*

- Request for quotation
- Changes in product requirements
- Procedures for reviewing contracts and purchase orders
- Product and service specifications
- Contract or accepted customer order

## *Examples of records*

- Evidence of ability to meet contract requirements
- Proof of contract and purchase order review
- Resolution of deviations from contract and purchase orders
- Results of product reviews and follow-up actions

### *Examples of processes that might be applicable*

- ➻ Sales/quoting
- ➻ Contract review
- ➻ Product and process design

### *Examples of linked processes*

- ➻ Manufacturing
- ➻ Business planning
- ➻ Purchasing
- ➻ Delivery
- ➻ Customer communication

### *Examples of performance measurements*

- ➻ Quotes submitted on time
- ➻ Quotes submitted versus contract awarded
- ➻ Budget to actual cost per contract
- ➻ Customer satisfaction

 **Pitfalls**

- ➻ No contract procedures exist
- ➻ Procedures are incomplete, misunderstood (often deliberately), or contradict each other, e.g., design versus sales versus production
- ➻ Records are inadequate or don't exist
- ➻ A lack of customer and/or supplier involvement

---

- No documented procedure for handling verbal orders

- Inadequate feedback of customer experience

- Undercommitted organization in which top management does not participate directly with customers and/or suppliers

- Not considering requirements for delivery and post-delivery activities

## Contract Review Process

### Process steps might include

- Give all affected parties the opportunity to review the contract

- Use a checklist to verify that all contract elements and acceptance criteria are included

- Provide for a way to make changes in the contract

- Reach agreement

- Discuss the results of the contract review

- Discuss the quality plan draft

### What to consider in the contract

- Reference to customer-specific requirements and product specifications

- Delivery information
  - Dates
  - Location

- ▶ Method of transit
- ▶ Packaging including labeling
- ▶ Product identification (batches, lots, material/part numbers, etc.)

↔ Responsibilities for
- ▶ Nonconforming product
- ▶ Product quality verification
- ▶ Contract review
- ▶ Resolution of differences (includes customer, organization, and suppliers)

↔ A service provider list that might contain
- ▶ Performance criteria
- ▶ Costs
- ▶ Profit margins
- ▶ Point of service infrastructure
- ▶ Technical skills
- ▶ Covered warranty items

# 7.3 Design and Development

7.3.1 Planning
7.3.2 Inputs
7.3.3 Outputs
7.3.4 Review
7.3.5 Verification
7.3.6 Validation
7.3.7 Control of Changes

## Why do it?

To make certain that your product meets all specified design requirements set by the customer, regulatory agencies, and statutory law.

## What is it?

Processes to control, verify, and validate product design and supporting software. A design control process has adequate resources and a structured approach to translate customer requirements into product specifications with measurable targets.

 **How do I do it?**

- Document all customer requirements and any other pertinent requirements (input). Lessons learned from previous projects is a tool many organizations use as a prevention tool for new projects. This can also include a bill of design, bill of materials, and bill of process (7.3.1)

- Establish a plan for design control and assign responsibilities. Design review and development review, verification and validation may be conducted separately or in any combination that works for the organization (7.3.1)

- Assign technically qualified staff; provide adequate resources with design tools and facilities conducive to innovative designs (7.3.2)

- Obtain input from all cross-functional, multidisciplinary technically competent teams and activities in order to establish and ensure

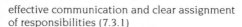

effective communication and clear assignment of responsibilities (7.3.1)

- ➧ Document the control procedures, with milestones with exit criteria as required by the Standard (7.3.1)

- ➧ Design output (7.3.3) to:
    - ➧ Meet input requirements
    - ➧ Contain reference data
    - ➧ Meet regulations and statutory law
    - ➧ Consider safety
    - ➧ Review documentation before release

- ➧ Provide output verification as planned (7.3.5) through:
    - ➧ Alternative calculations
    - ➧ Design tools
    - ➧ Comparison with proven design
    - ➧ Qualification tests
    - ➧ Review of documents before release (7.3.4)

- ➧ Validate the design
    - ➧ Develop a comprehensive validation plan and acceptance criteria (7.3.6)
    - ➧ Ensure that design verification is successful
    - ➧ Confirm final product meets design intent
    - ➧ Assess the need for multiple validations

- ➧ Develop change control procedures (7.3.7)
    - ➧ Identification

- Documentation; i.e., design change requests, drawing changes, feasibility studies

- Review

- Approvals based on change magnitude

## Example of documents

Documentation of procedures, responsibilities, and resources for design and development:

- Inputs and outputs (7.3.2, 7.3.3)

- Review and follow-up (7.3.4)

- Verification, i.e., modeling, simulations, etc. (7.3.5)

- Validation, i.e., design validation plan and report, finite element analysis, etc. (7.3.6)

- Changes, i.e., engineering work orders, etc. (7.3.7)

## Examples of records

- Group interface communications

- Input approval (7.3.2)

- Output verification (7.3.3)

- Review and follow up, i.e., design review based on test results, design review based on failure mode, etc. (7.3.4)

- Verification results and follow-up (7.3.5)

- Validation results and follow-up (7.3.6)

- Change approval (7.3.7)

### *Example of processes that might be applicable*

- Product design
- Process design
- Design review
- Design verification and design validation

### *Examples of linked processes*

- Sales/quoting
- Contract review
- Manufacturing
- Assembly
- Purchasing

### *Examples of performance measurements*

- Designs completed and submitted on time
- Number of design changes
- Success of verification and validation
- Manufacturing and assembly nonconformance related to design

 **Pitfalls**

- Design responsibilities/authorities/interfaces are not specified in writing, or are not followed
- Teams are not coordinated, especially between product and process responsibilities

- Drawings are not under control:
    - Irrational tolerances
    - Not checked or verified
    - Not authorized or no use of a change control system
    - Subjective descriptions on drawings
    - No evidence of review and approval
- There is a lack of real design reviews, e.g., system operated by one person, no discussions with manufacturing and assembly (individual invites participants by choice)
- A system exists but is not being used
- The tolerances that are specified are impossible to achieve, e.g., lack of production involvement, no design for manufacturability (DFM) or design for assembly (DFA) initiatives
- Prototypes are not subjected to critical examination
- Lack of solid modeling
- User publication requirements are not begun until design is almost complete
- Gauges and test equipment on development work are not calibrated
- Sampling systems are faulty or not agreed to by the customer

Stages in the Design Control Process

| Stage | Elements |
|---|---|
| **Design Planning** | ❑ Procedures for each activity established |
| | ❑ Responsibilities identified |
| | ❑ Resources adequate; qualified resources |
| | ❑ Interfaces between groups defined |
| | ❑ Communication between groups established |
| | ❑ Plans updated as design evolves |
| **Design Input** | ❑ Design requirements identified, including: |
| | ▶ Acceptance criteria |
| | ▶ Requirements of regulatory bodies |
| | ▶ Proper functioning |
| | ▶ Safety characteristics |
| | ❑ Adequacy reviewed |
| | ❑ Incomplete, ambiguous, or conflicting requirements resolved |
| **Design Output** | ❑ Technical documents to be used from production through servicing (drawings, specifications, instructions, and procedures) that are crucial to safe functioning of the product, including operation, storage, handling, maintenance, and disposal |
| | ❑ Output documents to be reviewed before release |

*Continued on next page*

| | |
|---|---|
| **Design Review** | ❑ Scheduled reviews of development status with all participating groups |
| | ❑ Record of reviews maintained |
| **Design Verification** | A plan to verify that output meets input. Techniques may include: |
| | ▶ Alternative calculations |
| | ▶ Comparison to other designs |
| | ▶ Tests and demonstrations |
| | ▶ Document review |
| **Design Validation** | A plan to validate that user needs and requirements are met. |
| | ❑ Follows successful verification |
| | ❑ Includes defined operating conditions |
| | ❑ Normally done on final product |
| | ❑ May have different validations for specific intended uses |
| **Design Change** | A plan to control design changes before implementation. |
| | ❑ Identify |
| | ❑ Document |
| | ❑ Review |
| | ❑ Approve |

## The difference between verification and validation:

•➤ Verification compares design output to input; it is the organization's point of view. For example, if the customer has ordered a lawn mower with a 22-inch blade and an engine with 5 hp, verify by checks and measures that these requirements have been met…

•➤ Validation ensures that the product meets user needs and requirements; it is the customer's point of view. In the lawn mower example, does the mower mow grass…?

## ✎ 7.4 Purchasing

7.4.1 Process

7.4.2 Information

7.4.3 Verification of Purchased Product

### Why do it?

To make certain the product received from your suppliers meets your requirements. You, in turn, incorporate this product into your production process to make the product that meets your customer's requirements. "Product" includes hardware, software, service, and processed materials.

### What is it?

A means to demonstrate effective operation of procedures for the purchasing process, which would include, as appropriate:

- Supplier evaluation
- Purchasing data
- Verification of purchased products at supplier's site
- Verification of purchased products at organization's site

*Reminder*: those who provide services (e.g., freight carriers, outside calibration services, special material processes such as heat treating, welding, coating, or plating) are suppliers, as well.

 *How do I do it?*

- Evaluate existing purchasing specifications and requirements
    - Review the process for developing and approving specifications
    - Update the procedures, if necessary

- Begin upgrading specifications as required. Prioritize criticality in meeting requirements

- Prepare, review, and approve purchasing documents
    - Refer to the updated specifications

- Establish criteria for determining supplier acceptability

- Evaluate and select suppliers based on their ability to meet requirements, including:
  - Product requirements (What is the supplier's product quality history?)
  - Delivery dependability including on-time, correct quality, and material, undamaged
  - Quality system capability (via audit/ISO 9001)

- Develop a supplier classification system
  - Many organizations develop a list of acceptable suppliers. An approved supplier list is not required by the Standards, but can be very useful. You must keep records of your approved suppliers.
  - Define the extent of control to be exercised over suppliers based on:
    - Type of product
    - Impact on final product quality
    - Results of previous quality audits
    - Previously demonstrated quality capability
    - Records of qualified suppliers should include providers of:
      - Raw materials
      - Special processes
      - Tooling
      - Equipment

- Business service, such as consultants and registrars (auditors)

➻ Establish a record system
  ➻ Keep records of your supplier's quality capability
  ➻ Established procedures for communicating requirements and performance with suppliers
  ➻ Results of periodic supplier review
  ➻ Purchase contracts and supporting data
  ➻ Review and approval of purchasing data

➻ Deploy the plan
  ➻ Develop a schedule
  ➻ Coordinate with receiving inspection
  ➻ Assign responsibility for administration

➻ Revise/improve procedures

➻ Evaluate revisions

### Examples of documents

- Purchasing information (7.4.2)
- Purchasing process procedures
- Product specifications
- List of acceptable suppliers

### Examples of records

- Results of purchasing evaluations and follow-up

- Supplier selection and acceptance criteria, including assessment of the supplier's capability and the effectiveness of the quality system

- Established procedures for communicating requirements and performance with suppliers, e.g., written documents, periodic visits, meetings

- Purchase contracts and supporting data

- Review and approval of purchasing data

### Examples of processes that might be applicable

- ✦ Purchasing
- ✦ Supplier selection and development
- ✦ Receiving

### Examples of performance measurements

- ✦ Purchased product received on time
- ✦ Quality of received product
- ✦ Premium freight incidents
- ✦ Damaged product
- ✦ Manufacturing nonconformance due to purchased product

 Pitfalls

- ✦ A lack of control or no evidence of control of suppliers
- ✦ No clear supplier performance criteria
- ✦ No records of acceptable suppliers
- ✦ You violate the rule of "We only buy from approved suppliers"
- ✦ Insufficient data on purchasing documents
- ✦ You do not inform suppliers of the quality system requirements when formalizing contracts
- ✦ You do not follow your own systems, e.g., a telephone order has no written confirmation

---

**PURCHASE ORDER**

Bill To: **d**

Ship To: **e**

| Quantity | Part # | Description | Cost/Unit | Total Cost |
|----------|--------|-------------|-----------|------------|
| **a** | **b** | **b** | **c** | **c** |
| | | | | |
| | | | | |
| | | | | |

Additional Comments: **f** **g** **h**

---

| | | | |
|---|---|---|---|
| (a) | Quantity | (f) | Packing instructions |
| (b) | Identification and description of the product | (g) | Requirements for approval of product, process, or personnel |
| (c) | Cost information | (h) | Requirements for product verification and release to the supplier |
| (d) | Billing instructions | | |
| (e) | Shipping instructions | | |

# 7.5 Production and Service Provisions

7.5.1 Control of Production and Service Provision

7.5.2 Validation of Processes for Production and Service Provision

7.5.3 Identification and Traceability

7.5.4 Customer Property

7.5.5 Preservation of Product

## Why do it?

To make certain that processes are carried out under controlled and verifiable conditions.

## What is it?

"Controlled conditions" include an understanding of the variation that exists in your processes. This includes common causes of variation and special causes of variation. A process "in control" has identified the special (also called assignable or non-random) causes of variation and taken steps to eliminate them. Many assignable causes of variation are attributable to personnel or machines/equipment. This is why the Standard specifically addresses work instructions for personnel and the maintenance and care of equipment.

Clause 7.5 calls for controlled conditions during production and service, including:

- ➡️ Information describing necessary product characteristics

- Work instructions, where needed
- Use and maintenance of suitable production equipment
- Suitable monitoring and measuring devices
- Monitoring activities
- Processes for release, delivery, and activities after delivery

 **How do I do it?**

Procedures are described in sub-clauses that in turn impose controls on all production processes.

### Post-delivery activities

**Note:** This section, referred to in ISO 9001:1994 as "servicing," has been included in *The Memory Jogger™* 9001:2008 for use by organizations that must fulfill contractual requirements after the customer has taken delivery of the product. Post-delivery activities are defined in Section 7.2.1.

### Why do it?

To ensure that after-sale attention is provided for your product, when required, to ensure complete customer satisfaction.

### What is it?

Processes to verify that post-delivery activities meet specified requirements. Because you need to treat servicing as an extension of your quality system, many or all of the sections of the Standard may apply.

**How do I do it?**

1. Identify customer service requirements.

2. Document the service requirements.

   ◆◆ Establish the needed activities to perform the service in a process map, flow chart, procedure or other method

   ◆◆ Perform the service

   ◆◆ Report and verify that the requirements are met

   ◆◆ Monitor customer satisfaction of these services

3. Revise and improve processes.

4. Evaluate revisions.

◆◆ Possible post-delivery activities:

   ◆◆ Recycling and/or final disposal

   ◆◆ Maintenance services (including tuning, adjusting, oiling, changing belts/hoses, etc.)

   ◆◆ Control of service manuals

   ◆◆ Training and certification of personnel

   ◆◆ Supply of service parts

   ◆◆ Corrective and preventive action of the service activities

   ◆◆ Auditing of service activities

   ◆◆ Management review of audit findings addressing the service activities

   ◆◆ Service records

### Examples of documents

- ➡ Servicing requirements
- ➡ Service agreements
- ➡ Servicing procedures and manuals
- ➡ Service personnel certified technical training requirements
- ➡ Measurement equipment and calibration procedures

### Examples of records

- ➡ Personnel training results and certifications
- ➡ Measurement equipment and calibration results
- ➡ Corrective and preventive action records
- ➡ Service records
- ➡ Process validation, as required (see sub-clause 7.5.2)

### *Examples of processes that might be applicable*

- Manufacturing
- Perishable tool management
- Fluid management
- Calibration
- Preventive maintenance
- Monitoring and measurement of processes and product
- Delivery
- Service

### *Linked processes*

- Sales/quoting
- Product and process design
- Purchasing
- Non-conforming product
- Product warranty
- Corrective action
- Preventive action
- Customer satisfaction

##  Pitfalls

- A lack of liaison between the service department and the main company
- No defined methods for providing the service(s)

- Defined methods are incomplete
- Field measurement equipment is inadequate compared to equipment used in the factory
- Technical incompetence

# 7.5.2 Validation of Processes for Production and Service Provision

### Why do it?

Processes are to be validated to ensure they accomplish what they are intended to do, especially in situations where it may not be possible to verify quality by checking later.

### What is it?

A plan to provide assurance that process controls are sufficient to ensure meeting all customer requirements.

 ### How do I do it?

➡ Identify all process factors (potential variables) that may affect the capability of the product or service to meet customer requirements (i.e., process failure modes and effects analysis (PFMEA), Ppk, DFM, DFA studies, etc.)

➡ Ensure that all equipment requirements are identified and that equipment and facilities meet performance requirements

➡ Verify that operation and administration requirements of each production process have been verified

➡ Confirm that adequate training is available for all personnel and that personnel are competent

➡ Verify that documented procedures are adequate for all production requirements and situations

➡ Ensure adequate record keeping to demonstrate that procedural controls are being followed

➡ Provide for process revalidation when there is a significant change in product or production method

### Examples of documents

- ♦ Listing of potentially variable factors affecting the process:
  - ▶ Materials
  - ▶ Operation
  - ▶ Environment
  - ▶ Utilities
  - ▶ Logistics and transportation suppliers
- ♦ Training criteria required for qualified personnel and competence requirements
- ♦ Work instructions
- ♦ Clearly define how to implement and verify all approved processes and controls (parameters)

### Examples of records

- ♦ Record of continuous monitoring and control of critical process characteristics
- ♦ Evidence of analysis of process, equipment, and personnel records
- ♦ Records of validation and revalidation
- ♦ Analysis of customer usage to identify opportunities for improved process control (see 8.2.1)

### *Examples of processes that might be applicable*

- ➤ Validation of processes
- ➤ Maintenance of equipment, perhaps using both preventive and predictive methods

### *Linked processes*

- ➤ Manufacturing
- ➤ Product and process design
- ➤ Production equipment maintenance
- ➤ Calibration
- ➤ Corrective action
- ➤ Customer communication

### *Examples of performance measurements*

- ➤ Validations completed on time
- ➤ Customer feedback related to "special processes"
- ➤ Manufacturing nonconformance related to "special processes"

##  Pitfalls

- ➤ Overlooking factors that are essential to meeting customer requirements, such as adequate equipment and personnel training requirements
- ➤ A lack of demonstrable planning for control of personnel, machines, materials, methods of work, environment, etc.

- No objectives have been set for product or project
- Inadequate planning for validation and verification
- Inadequate written work instructions/procedures, where their absence could affect quality

## 7.5.3 Identification and Traceability

### Why do it?

To make certain that your product is properly identified and is traceable to the raw materials that went into all stages of production, and to avoid errors that can cause scrap and rework.

### What is it?

A provision for identifying incoming materials, in-process product, and finished product. Where required, it is a record that tracks the history, usage, and location of product.

- **Identification:** The ability to separate two or more materials or products, i.e., How do you tell product A from B from C, etc.? This is especially crucial if the products visibly appear to be the same

- **Traceability:** The ability to separate material or product by individual unit, batch, lot, or run. Traceability allows you to trace issues back to a supplier or forward to a customer for a recall or other traceability issues

### ⟨?⟩ *How do I do it?*

- ↪ Establish customer and/or regulatory requirements, i.e., *hazardous materials or their disposal.*

- ↪ Document existing traceability practices, including:
    - ↪ From your supplier
    - ↪ In your plant or to your customer
    - ↪ At/after installation

- ↪ Revise/improve traceability procedures.
    - ↪ Including statutory and regulatory requirements

- ↪ Consider types of identification to provide traceability, for product history and application, as well as location:
    - ↪ Unit identification (serial number)
    - ↪ SKU or UPC number(s)
    - ↪ Lot identification
    - ↪ Production date code

- ↪ Consider methods of identification:
    - ↪ Paper versus electronic
    - ↪ Labeling or bar codes
    - ↪ Etching

- ↪ Determine the following about the records kept:
    - ↪ Availability
    - ↪ Organization
    - ↪ Indexing
    - ↪ Retention times
    - ↪ Responsibility

### Examples of documents

Procedures for product and lot identification at all stages, such as:

- Receiving activity
- Certificate of Acceptance (COA)
- Production
- Final product acceptance
- Warehousing and distribution
- Material management
- Product lists
- Production and/or service parts

### Examples of records

Material batches, lots, or units at all stages, such as:

- Receiving
- Production
- Final product acceptance
- Warehousing and distribution

### *Examples of processes that might be applicable*

- ●▸ Identification and traceability
- ●▸ Receiving
- ●▸ Manufacturing
- ●▸ Transportation and logistics
- ●▸ Material management
- ●▸ Inspecting and testing

### *Examples of linked processes*

- ●▸ Process design
- ●▸ Calibration
- ●▸ Purchasing

### *Examples of performance measurements*

- ●▸ Monitoring and measurement status identified
- ●▸ Inbound raw material compliance
- ●▸ Nonconformance due to unidentified or suspect product

## Pitfalls

- ●▸ Components, materials, or products are unmarked
- ●▸ Internal material tagging is inconsistently implemented
- ●▸ Batches are stacked on top of each other, when batch identity is required
- ●▸ A stage or operation is missing, when traceability is necessary

| Term | Definition | Graphic Example |
|---|---|---|
| Identification | Ability to separate two or more materials or products. | 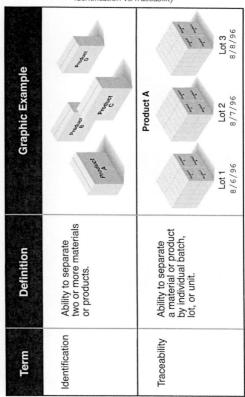 |
| Traceability | Ability to separate a material or product by individual batch, lot, or unit. | |

Adapted from *Demystifying ISO 9000*, Information
Mapping's Guide to the ISO 9000 Standards, p. 2-32

## 7.5.4 Customer Property

### Why do it?

To make certain that the property you receive from your customers will be incorporated into your product and ultimately meet all of your customers' requirements. To ensure you protect and safeguard any customer property including as appropriate: equipment, returnable packaging, and intellectual/confidential property.

### What is it?

Methods for verification, storage, preservation and maintenance of customer-owned property. The requirement to provide acceptable product is implied.

 **How do I do it?**

→ Determine the existence of customer property (including test equipment, packaging, labels, drawings, raw materials, sub-assemblies, etc.). This would include property provided to your organization to be incorporated into your product.

Your customer, in this case, serves as your supplier. Examples:

- → Customer labels or logo emblems for attachment to your product, or customer packaging furnished for your product

- → Printed instructions and/or accessories for inclusion with your packaged product

- Tooling provided by your customer
- Test and inspection equipment provided by your customer, for your use in product verification or validation
- A service, such as your use of your customer's delivery service
- Prints, drawings, and other customer-owned documents

- Establish practice for
  - Verification
  - Storage
  - Handling
  - Preservation
  - Maintenance
  - Labeling or suitable identification—tooling, equipment and returnable packaging

- Revise/improve your procedures

- Evaluate revisions

### Examples of documents

- ◆ Instructions for verification of storage and handling process, and maintenance process

- ◆ Instructions for controlling non-conformances

### Examples of records

- ◆ Receipt and verification results

- ◆ Certificates of Acceptance (COAs)

- ◆ Rejected product (lost, damaged, unusable)

- ◆ Product inventory records

- ◆ Reports to customers

### Examples of processes that might be applicable

- ◆ Customer communication

- ◆ Protection of customer property

- ◆ Material management

### Examples of linked processes

- ◆ Customer satisfaction

- ◆ Maintenance

- ◆ Contract review

- ◆ Manufacturing

- Product design
- Dunnage preservation

### *Examples of performance measurements*

- Customer satisfaction results
- Maintenance on customer tooling/equipment completed on time
- Reporting of problems to the customer on time
- Damaged or lost container/dunnage

 **Pitfalls**

- Items are damaged or badly stored
- Containers aren't returned from ship to location in a timely manner
- Poorly designed containers resulting in material damage
- Storage area does not protect customer property, i.e., dirt, corrosion, moisture, etc.
- Customer-owned property is not adequately identified
- Assuming that the customer has given you the materials, equipment, etc., but not having documentation to verify this

# 7.5.5 Preservation of Product

## Why do it?

To make certain that your processes for identification, handling, storage, packaging, preservation, protection, and delivery of product are adequate, and to protect the integrity of product at all stages. This also applies to constituent parts of a product.

## What is it?

Adequate processes at all stages, such as:

→→ Incoming materials

→→ In-process product

→→ Finished product

→→ Conditions during delivery, as specified by the customer

→→ Prevention of damage or deterioration

→→ Secure storage and appropriate receipt and dispatch methods

→→ Packaging, packing, and marking processes

→→ Methods for preserving and segregating products

→→ Protection of product after inspection and test during storage and during delivery to destination

**How do I do it?**

- ✦ Identify the critical points in the process, i.e., contamination risk, harsh environmental conditions

- ✦ Review available information, e.g., damage rates, shelf life

- ✦ Generate methods for:
    - ✦ Packaging designs
    - ✦ Unique customer packaging requirements
    - ✦ In-processes handling
    - ✦ Packaging, packing, and marking
    - ✦ Storage

- ✦ Container retrieval using protective techniques
    - ✦ Inventory/stock management processes
    - ✦ Transportation techniques/carrier selection
    - ✦ Storage, preservation, protection, and segregation methods
    - ✦ Environmental impact

- ✦ Revise and improve processes
    - ✦ Improving contamination and damage protection methods

- ✦ Evaluate revisions
    - ✦ Assessing container preservation effectiveness and making improvements when these methods demonstrate deterioration

### Examples of documents

- ↪ Handling processes

- ↪ Storage processes, including receipt and dispatch authorizations

### Inventory documents

- ↪ Preservation requirements

- ↪ Packaging requirements

- ↪ Packaging, labels, and shipping container formats

- ↪ Delivery requirements

### Examples of records

- ↪ Verification of storage condition

- ↪ Storage dates and expiration dates

- ↪ Delivery dates as needed

- ↪ Verification results on method of delivery

### Examples of processes that might be applicable

- ↪ Inventory (FIFO, etc.)

- ↪ Storage (special customer specific controls for custom dunnage)

### Examples of linked processes

- ↪ Manufacturing

- Identification and traceability
- Material handling
- Work environment
- Facilities maintenance

### *Examples of performance measurements*

- Damaged product
- Obsolete product found in inventory
- Damaged product to customer

 Pitfalls

- Procedures and preservation controls are inadequate, obsolete, or unclear
- Procedures do not address in-coming or work in progress, nor final product
- Materials are:
    - Damaged/corroded
    - Overage
    - Shortage
    - Unprotected
    - Unidentified
    - Lost
    - Stolen
    - Nonconforming
- Lack of security; free access to a large inventory
- Products damaged in delivery to customer

| Identification | Examples of product, packaging, and master carton marking, as required or needed:<br>❑ Serial number<br>❑ Date code<br>❑ Regulatory marking requirements<br>❑ Linkage to test and inspection records<br>❑ Traceability (see sub-clause 7.5.3) |
|---|---|
| Handling | ❑ Protect the product using containers, pallets, or work platforms<br>❑ Install and maintain conveyors and other automated transfer systems for product protection<br>❑ Train operators in awareness of product protection<br>❑ Operate lift trucks, loaders, and other vehicles in a safe manner to minimize damage |
| Packaging | ❑ Develop unit pack and master packs to provide appropriate protection while in organization's plant and during shipping |
| Storage | ❑ Provide adequate space and facilities<br>❑ Ensure cleanliness<br>❑ Maintain an appropriate temperature and humidity<br>❑ Provide appropriate security and access to storage areas<br>❑ Provide for appropriate identification marking and traceability |
| Protection | ❑ Control the temperature and humidity<br>❑ Segregate product where necessary |
| Delivery | ❑ Provide for proper protection after release until organization is no longer responsible for distribution handling, per contract<br>❑ Consider the delivery method<br>❑ Control the temperature and humidity<br>❑ Provide security during delivery |

Adapted from *Demystifying ISO 9000*, Information Mapping's Guide to the ISO 9000 Standards, p. 2-56

# ⚙️ 7.6 Control of Monitoring and Measuring Equipment

## Why do it?

To make certain that inspection, measuring, and test equipment is capable of consistently providing specified measurement requirements that, when implemented, are reproducible and repeatable, so that proper decisions can be made for control and acceptance of product.

## What is it?

Process to ensure the organization has determined monitoring and measurements to be carried out and monitoring and measuring equipment that will provide evidence of conformity of the product to requirements has been property chosen. In addition, the monitoring and measurement equipment must be calibrated and remain so. Also, it is the assurance that measurement uncertainty is known and consistent with required measurement capability.

 ## How do I do it?

Refer to ISO 10012-1 and ISO 10012-2, "Quality Assurance Requirements for Measuring Equipment."

↦ Identify all inspection and test requirements

   ↦ Measurements to be made

   ↦ Measurement equipment capability and variation

   ↦ Accuracy requirements

- ↔ List equipment and software available to conduct inspections/tests (fixed and portable)
  - ↔ Laboratory equipment
  - ↔ Inspection and test equipment
  - ↔ Production machinery
  - ↔ Jigs, fixtures, templates
  - ↔ Test software
- ↔ Identify recognized calibration requirements and verification procedures for each piece of equipment
  - ↔ Fixed and portable equipment
  - ↔ Required measurement capability
  - ↔ Known measurement uncertainty
  - ↔ Calibration schedules
- ↔ Review and flowchart existing procedures and documentation for:
  - ↔ Measurements to be made
  - ↔ Measurement precision and accuracy
  - ↔ Calibration procedures
  - ↔ Measurement uncertainty
  - ↔ Identification of calibration status on equipment
  - ↔ Out-of-calibration action
  - ↔ Work environment control
  - ↔ Handling, storage, preservation, and retrieval
  - ↔ Safeguarding against unauthorized adjustment

- ◆◆ Rechecking intervals
- ◆◆ Revise/improve methods, including any procedures or work instructions
    - ◆◆ Based on measurement equipment performance and associated calibration intervals
- ◆◆ Consider hard copy versus electronic records
- ◆◆ Establish an effective record system
    - ◆◆ Includes "as-found" and "as-left" controls
    - ◆◆ Calibration masters that are customer approved or are directly linked to an international standard
- ◆◆ Evaluate revisions

### Examples of documents

- ➜ Required measurements and their accuracy

- ➜ Listing of all measurement, inspection, and test equipment affecting quality

- ➜ Basis for calibration (customer approved process or a national standard)

- ➜ Calibration procedure

- ➜ Software verification process

- ➜ Corrective action procedure

- ➜ Verification and calibration schedule

### Example of records

- ➜ Calibration and verification results

- ➜ Measurement equipment repairs or replacements

*Examples of processes that might be applicable*

- Monitoring and measurement
- Calibration
- Preventive maintenance
- Protection of equipment
- Measurement equipment supplier performance

*Examples of linked processes*

- Manufacturing
- Process design
- Corrective action

 **Pitfalls**

- No real control system
- No one is responsible for operating the system
- Equipment that should be in the system is not in the system (particularly in research and development areas)
- Equipment is not identified
- Equipment is not stored or handled to protect the equipment from damage
- No traceability to a national or international standard

- Measurement system masters are not controlled and/or need replacement

- Failure to ensure that adjustable equipment is not altered to invalidate calibration

- When equipment is found to be out of calibration, no assessment is made on the impact on previous results

# Chapter
# EIGHT

# MEASUREMENT, ANALYSIS AND IMPROVEMENT

8.1 General ................................................. 189

8.2 Monitoring and Measurement ............... 190

    8.2.1 Customer Satisfaction

    8.2.2 Internal Audit

    8.2.3 Monitoring and Measurement of Processes

    8.2.4 Monitoring and Measurement of Product

8.3 Control of Nonconforming Product.......... 208

8.4 Analysis of Data .................................212

8.5 Improvement ..................................... 216

    8.5.1 Continual Improvement

    8.5.2 Corrective Action

    8.5.3 Preventive Action

# ⚗️ What's changed from ISO 9001:2000?

●→ Note added about monitoring customer perception (8.2.1)

●→ Addition of word "The" to selection of auditors; Reworded paragraph about documented procedure; now states "management...shall ensure any necessary corrections and corrective actions..."; Note changed to reflect ISO 19011 (8.2.2)

●→ Addition of a note about determining suitable methods (8.2.3)

●→ Rearranged first two paragraphs; reworded last paragraph (8.2.4)

●→ Reworded sentence about documented procedure; added the words "where applicable" to paragraph about dealing with nonconforming product; added bullet d (8.3)

●→ Changed reference to 7.2.1 in bullet b to 8.2.4; Reference to 8.2.3 and 8.2.4 in bullet c; reference to suppliers 7.4 in bullet d (8.4)

●→ Addition of "effectiveness" to bullet f (8.5.2)

●→ Addition of "effectiveness" to bullet e (8.5.3)

# 8.1. General

## *Why do it?*

To make certain that monitoring and measurement processes and activities needed to ensure conformity and accomplish improvement are defined, planned, and implemented.

## *What is it?*

Demonstration that a plan for measuring, analyzing, and continually improving your processes and product service exists and is in operation. This includes making use of statistical and process improvement techniques.

##  *How do I do it?*

Define, plan, and implement the requirements listed in the remaining portions of clause 8. These include:

- ⤢ Monitoring, measurement and analysis of:
  - ▶ Customer satisfaction
  - ▶ QMS (internal audit)
  - ▶ Processes
  - ▶ Product
- ⤢ Control of nonconformity
- ⤢ Analysis of data
- ⤢ Continual improvement in effectiveness of the QMS

- Corrective action
- Preventive action
- Use of statistical tools
- Use of process improvement tools such as modeling, value stream mapping, lean enterprise initiatives, etc.

## 8.2 Monitoring and Measurement

8.2.1 Customer Satisfaction
8.2.2 Internal Audit
8.2.3 Monitoring and Measurement of Processess
8.2.4 Monitoring and Measurement of Product

### Why do it?

To make certain that the total of all efforts to meet customer requirements is actually resulting in satisfied customers.

### What is it?

An action plan to search out and put to use information that reflects the degree of satisfaction as perceived by your customers.

 How do I do it?

- Reference the requirements called for in 7.2
- Customer-related processes, and 7.2.3 with customer communication, in particular

↔ Establish a process for compiling, analyzing, and acting upon information contained in customer feedback data, reflecting the level of customer satisfaction (8.4)

↔ Incorporate customer satisfaction measures into continual improvement efforts (8.5)

Performance indicators may include:

- ↔ Quality of delivered parts
- ↔ Quality of inbound materials
- ↔ Field returns
- ↔ Delivery performance, such as premium freight
- ↔ Notifications to customers concerning quality of delivery
- ↔ Manufacturing processes effectiveness and efficiency
- ↔ Warranty data
- ↔ Supplier performance

↔ Seek additional sources of information, reflecting the perception of customer satisfaction, appropriate to your type of business. This may include service calls, product returns, repair parts usage, changes in market share, and downtime affecting customers

↔ Consider practicality of conducting customer satisfaction surveys and using interviews with customers and consumers. These surveys can be mailed or posted on the organization's web site

•• In cases where your product is used by your customers as a component of their product, consider working with your immediate customers to develop feedback from later production or distribution stages. Consider internal as well as external customers

### Examples of documents

- •• Procedures for retrieving, analyzing, and acting on customer complaint or warranty data

- •• Procedures for conducting surveys of customer satisfaction/dissatisfaction

- •• Procedures for analyzing and acting upon other measures of customer satisfaction/dissatisfaction

### Examples of records

- •• Rate of customer returns and complaints for quality reasons

- •• Record of actions taken in response to problems identified through customer satisfaction data

- •• Product service and repair records

### Process that might be applicable

- •• Customer satisfaction
- •• Internal customer satisfaction

- Customer complaint process
- Warranty analysis and actions

### *Examples of linked processes*
- Customer communication
- Continual improvement
- Corrective actions
- Management review
- Analysis of data

### *Examples of performance measurements*
- On-time delivery to customer
- PPM
- Incidents of premium freight
- Inbound material over/short or damaged
- Outbound damaged product

 **Pitfalls**
- No process for obtaining and acting upon customer complaints/returns
- Overlooking available data reflecting customer satisfaction
- Not using information gained to continually improve products and processes
- No returned goods or warranty analysis process

# 8.2.2 Internal Audit

## Why do it?

To make certain that your quality activities meet requirements and demonstrate the effectiveness of your QMS. This strives to ensure the continued capability of all business management system processes.

## What is it?

A plan with documented procedure(s) for conducting internal audits of your QMS.

→→ Schedule audits according to status and importance of activity

→→ Carry out audits using the process approach (see the turtle tool in Chapter 2 for an example of a tool that can be used to audit processes) with independent personnel

→→ Document audit results and any follow-up

→→ Communicate audit results to appropriate personnel, including management

→→ Initiate corrective action

→→ Verify and record effectiveness of the corrective action taken

 ## How do I do it?

Refer to ISO 19011 "Guidelines for Environmental and Quality Auditing".

- Identify the activities to be audited

  Base the audit plan on an audit schedule that can be adjusted depending on product and process performance

- Establish the qualifications of audit personnel, including:

  - Experience
  - Training
  - Skills
  - Availability
  - Independence
  - Meet requirements of competence (6.2.2)

- Develop (or update) audit procedures to include:

  - Planning
  - Responsibilities
  - Requirements
  - Records
  - Report of results
  - Working environment

- Conduct an initial quality audit

  - Evaluate the adequacy of defined processes
  - Determine the effectiveness of the processes
  - Evaluate competence of internal auditors
  - Determine the suitability of the working environment

- Establish a permanent quality audit program
    - QMS audit to verify compliance:
        - to the Standard
        - to additional organization and customer-specific QMS requirements
        - by using process-based checklists
    - Audit plans should cover your entire system. Cover all processes and, if you use more than one shift or crew, include all shifts and crews

### Examples of processes that might be applicable

- Internal audit
- Management reviews, results, and actions
- Selection and evaluation of auditors

### Example of linked processes

- Corrective action
- Analysis of data
- Management review
- Internal communication

### Example of performance measurements

- Internal audits completed on time
- Corrective actions completed on time and verified as being effective

### Examples of documents

- ➢ Internal audit schedule
- ➢ Procedures for conducting an internal audit
- ➢ List of qualified auditors
- ➢ Documented procedure that defines responsibilities and requirements for planning and conducting audits, establishing audit records, and reporting results
- ➢ Auditor-prepared open-ended questions based on process performance

### Examples of records

- ➢ Results of internal audits
- ➢ Record of management audit review
- ➢ Record of corrective action taken
- ➢ Competence of auditor, including evaluations and reevaluations

# 🔱 Pitfalls

- ➥ Auditing to elements rather than to the process approach
- ➥ Inadequate auditor resources
- ➥ No audit nonconformance corrective action verification process
- ➥ No system exists
- ➥ No corrective action on findings
- ➥ Auditors are not adequately trained or are not competent
- ➥ No independent person is present to conduct the audit
- ➥ Documents and records are incomplete

## *Establishing an Internal Quality Audit Process*

- ➥ Develop an overall audit plan
- ➥ Assign audit personnel
- ➥ Schedule audits on the basis of performance, importance, and status of the given process
- ➥ Review the effectiveness of any previous corrective action
- ➥ Conduct the audit
- ➥ Submit the audit report to management
- ➥ Management to review any noncompliance
- ➥ Management to take corrective action on non-compliances

•• Follow up on top management corrective actions for effective implementation

### Checks and Balances to Ensure Continued Effective Use of ISO 9001:2008

After your company is registered to ISO 9001:2008, your organization must ensure that the requirements continue to be met. Three activities provide for this continuance:

- •• Internal audits (sub-clause 8.2.2)
- •• Periodic management review (sub-clause 5.6)
- •• Scheduled surveillance audits by the 2nd party auditor (if needed) and 3rd party registrar auditor(s)

## 8.2.3 Monitoring and Measurement of Processes

### Why do it?

To make certain that processes conform to all requirements at each production stage, to identify nonconforming processes at the earliest possible stage, and to facilitate corrective action and continual improvement.

To understand why a particular process is performing at a certain level and why it may be underperforming.

### What is it?

Demonstrates that process-monitoring and process-control procedures are in operation to ensure that product meets intended purpose.

###  How do I do it?

→ Evaluate the monitoring and measurement needs of each stage in the realization process

→ Consider alternative monitoring and measurement methods appropriate for each stage. Refer to resource materials on improving work processes, flowcharting, process control, and process capability in Chapter 2

→ Put into use selected appropriate monitoring and measurement procedures. Provide for adequate administration, training, and documentation

*Some examples might be*:

→ Verify process capability of all new and existing manufacturing processes, using process studies. Document with specifications for production, measurement, and maintenance instructions, with objectives for achieving appropriate:

▶ Process capability

▶ Reliability

▶ Maintainability

▶ Availability

▶ Acceptance criteria

- ◆◆ Maintain process capability to ensure conformance to:
    - ▶ measurement method
    - ▶ sampling plans
    - ▶ acceptance criteria
    - ▶ reaction plans when needed, involving:
        - - Containment
        - - 100% inspection
        - - Corrective action plan
        - - Timing
        - - Responsibilities
        - - Making processes stable and capable
        - - Review with customer when required
    - ◆◆ Date of process changes to be recorded
- ◆◆ Continually improve practices and processes
- ◆◆ Evaluate process revisions

### Examples of documents

- ◆◆ Process for determining a need and correct selection of the particular statistical technique
- ◆◆ Listing of applications of statistical techniques

### Example of records

- ◆◆ Results of statistical techniques that are applied

### *Example of processes that might be applicable*

- Measurement and examples of processes
- Calibration
- Corrective actions
- Non-conforming product
- Manufacturing

### *Example of performance measurement techniques*

- Cpk
- Anova
- Weibull and regression analysis
- X-Bar and R

##  Pitfalls

- Not using the correct statistical technique
- Ineffective use of statistical methods
- Statistical technique incompetence
- Ineffective use of sampling systems
- Over-control or over adjustments to a particular process

## Typical Applications of Statistical Methods

- Process-control and process-capability studies
- Determination of quality levels in sampling plans
- Data analysis, performance assessment, and non-conformity analysis

- Process improvement
- Safety evaluation and risk analysis
- Trend identification
- Cause–effect relationship identification
- Design of experiments and factorial analysis, to identify variables
- Analysis of variance and regression analysis, to provide quantitative process models
- Tests of significance, for decision making
- Quality control charts and Cumulative Sum Chart (CUSUM) techniques for monitoring, control, and measurement
- Statistical sampling, for acceptance and cost control
- Graphical methods, for diagnosis

## 8.2.4 Monitoring and Measurement of Product

### Why do it?
To make certain that the product conforms to requirements at each production stage, to identify nonconforming product at the earliest possible stage, and to facilitate and verify corrective action effectiveness and continual improvement.

### What is it?
Demonstrates that inspection and test procedures are in operation to ensure that the product conforms to specified requirements. These may include:

- ✦ Incoming product
    - ▶ Procedures for inspection and verification
    - ▶ Holding or controlling until verified
    - ▶ The amount that you do depends upon the level of supplier control
- ✦ In-process product
    - ▶ Procedures for identifying and inspecting product
    - ▶ Positive control until tests are complete
- ✦ Finished product
    - ▶ Procedures to ensure that inspections and tests are completed
    - ▶ Product conforms to requirements
    - ▶ Product is not released until tests are completed

 *How do I do it?*

- ✦ Establish a separate plan or procedure for each of the following that apply:
    - ✦ Receiving inspection and testing (consider the existing level of supplier control)
    - ✦ Layout inspection
    - ✦ Functional testing
    - ✦ In-process inspection and testing
    - ✦ Final inspection and testing
- ✦ Determine the policy, e.g., *Do not use until verified*

- Identify categories of the product that are affected, i.e., work-in-process, finished product, etc.

- List all internal and external quality requirements that are subject to inspection and test

    - Establish requirements

    - Measurements to be made, i.e., key part characteristics or process parameters

    - How to measure, i.e., choosing the right measurement equipment

    - Skills required

- Ensure that the procedures for identifying specified requirements are available, including any customer specific requirements

- Provide for complete and current procedures at the point of inspection/test

    - Sufficiently frequent inspection intervals

    - Available to customers

- Provide for positive product identification/recall for urgent release by linking the product to the approved release level

- Release product only when successful tests/records are complete

- Revise/improve procedures by ensuring procedures include all recall and product return requirements

- Evaluate revision

## *Examples of documents*

- → Procedures for test and inspection criteria for:
    - ▶ Receiving inspection and testing
    - ▶ In-process inspection and testing
    - ▶ Final inspection and testing
- → Final inspector competency criteria clearly defined

## *Examples of records*

- → Test results of inspection and testing
    - ▶ Incoming
    - ▶ In-process
    - ▶ Final
- → Responsible authority for release noted in approved process description or procedure along with release authority

## *Example of processes that might be applicable*

- ◆◆ Manufacturing
- ◆◆ Product design
- ◆◆ Determination of customer requirements

## *Example of linked processes*

- ◆◆ Delivery
- ◆◆ Customer satisfaction
- ◆◆ Nonconforming product
- ◆◆ Corrective action

## *Examples of performance measurements*

- ◆◆ PPM
- ◆◆ Customer complaints
- ◆◆ Warranty issues
- ◆◆ Returned product
- ◆◆ Rework
- ◆◆ Scrap

 **Pitfalls**

- ◆◆ A lack of control at receiving, e.g., material that requires testing/inspection goes directly to inventory
- ◆◆ Material that is released to production is neither identified nor under complete control
- ◆◆ Specified inspections or tests are not carried out

- Records of inspection or test are missing
- Final inspection or test is bypassed, or company product release procedures are bypassed
- Reworked product is not fully re-inspected

# 8.3 Control of Nonconforming Product

## Why do it?

To make certain that you do not use or unintentionally deliver nonconforming product to your customer.

## What is it?

Procedures in operation that will help you:

- Identify nonconforming product
- Evaluate degree and extent of the nonconformance
- Segregate product physically, where practical, or through clear identification
- Define who is responsible for authorizing disposition
  - ▶ Dispose of nonconforming product according to the quality plan or procedures. Authorize disposition according to:
    - Rework to meet specification and reinspect material before further processing

- Repair to make fit for use, but not as designed, along with evidence of customer acceptance

- Acceptance for use, with or without repair

- Regrade for another application

- Reject or scrap

- Notify concerned parties such as customer, supplier, and organizational material management

 **How do I do it?**

↦ Review and document your procedures for:

  ↦ Identification

  ↦ Documentation

  ↦ Control

  ↦ Segregation

  ↦ Prevention of inadvertent use/installation

↦ Document the procedures for disposition, notification, and classification

↦ Assign authority for material disposition approval

↦ Document the procedures for reinspection of repairs or rework

  ↦ Rework produces an item that is in every way indistinguishable from a "first-time-through" acceptable

- ► Repair makes the item meet requirements but is different in some way, e.g., welded, from the original design. Repair often requires customer approval or concession, before acceptance

- ►► Document any concession reporting and handling procedures by clearly defining accounting rules, and required records

- ►► Revise and approve your procedures

- ►► Evaluate revisions

### Examples of documents

- ►► Nonconformity control activities

- ►► Statement of responsibility for review and authority for disposition of nonconforming product

- ►► Documented procedure for control of nonconforming product

- ►► Statement in contract on authority for acceptance by waiver concession or repair

### Examples of records

- ►► Results of investigation and disposition of nonconformance

- ►► Reinspection of reworked or repaired product

- ►► Notification of concerned parties

- ►► Agreements of acceptance of waiver concessions

### Examples of processes that might be applicable

- Nonconforming product
- Rework
- Waivers/deviation permit process
- Material management
- Financial management

### Example of linked processes

- Corrective action
- Manufacturing
- Analysis of data
- Identification

### Example of performance measurements

- Rework
- Repair
- Scrap
- PPM

 **Pitfalls**

- Nonconforming material is not identified, or is being held in a nonspecified area

- There is no defined responsibility for review and disposition of rework

- There is no specified rework process or requirements

- Repair or rework is not reinspected prior to release back into the manufacturing process

# 8.4 Analysis of Data

**Why do it?**

To make certain that your QMS is effective and efficient, and that you have identified places in your process where the collection and analysis of data is necessary to ensure quality, to detect potential problems, and to target improvement opportunities.

**What is it?**

A process for identifying the need to collect data that will enable you to understand process behavior and establish, control, and verify process capability and product quality. Where the need is established, you must maintain and document procedures for data collection, analysis, resulting improvements, and associated verification activities.

**How do I do it?**

- Identify existing applications and procedures for:
    - Establishing process capability
    - Identifying potential problems
    - Verifying product characteristics and process parameters
- Evaluate correctness and effectiveness of data collection to:
    - Demonstrate suitability of QMS
    - Measure customer satisfaction

- ◆ Determine conformance to requirements
- ◆ Identify ways to continually improve by defect prevention, variation, and waste reduction
- ◆ Identify opportunities for preventive action
- ◆ Make use of data from other sources
- ◆ Analyze and use data to:
  - ◆ Address customer related problems (8.2.1)
  - ◆ Ensure conformity to product requirements (8.2.4)
  - ◆ Identify trends to aid review, decisions, and planning (8.2.3 and 8.2.4)
  - ◆ Improve supplier conformance (7.4)
- ◆ Examine the quality plan, manufacturing control plan, and routings for additional value added improvements
- ◆ Evaluate the effectiveness and efficiency of any new applications

### Examples of documents

- Process for determining a need for data collection and analysis applications

- Listing of applications and their linkages to all product realization processes (customer, organizational, and supplier)

### Examples of records

- Results of statistical techniques and recommended actions

- Performance data on the QMS

### Examples of processes that might be applicable

- Data analysis

- Root cause analysis

- Statistical analysis

- Continual improvement

### *Example of linked processes*

- ↠ Non-conforming product
- ↠ Corrective action
- ↠ Purchasing
- ↠ Management reviews
- ↠ Marketing and sales

### *Example of performance measurements*

- ↠ Completed continual improvements
- ↠ Timely reporting to management reviews
- ↠ Lessons learned applied to future projects
- ↠ Measurement system performance
- ↠ Ongoing process capability
- ↠ Ongoing supply chain performance

 **Pitfalls**

- ↠ Not analyzing data when necessary
- ↠ Not understanding product or process data
- ↠ Ineffective use of analytical methods
  - ▶ Collecting data that no one uses
  - ▶ Not using the data collected to continually improve processes of the organization

## Typical applications of data collection and analysis

- ➼ Market analysis

- ➼ Product design

- ➼ Dependability specification, longevity, and durability prediction

- ➼ Process-control and process-capability studies

- ➼ Determination of quality levels in sampling plans

- ➼ Data analysis, performance assessment, and nonconformity analysis

- ➼ Process improvement

- ➼ Safety evaluation and risk analysis

- ➼ Trend identification

- ➼ Cause–effect relationship identification


## ➼ 8.5 Improvement

8.5.1 Continual improvement

8.5.2 Corrective action

8.5.3 Preventive action


### Why do it?

To make certain that there is an active plan for continual business management system improvements, and that causes of nonconforming product are investigated, specifically to eliminate these nonconformances. You should also attempt to detect and eliminate potential causes of nonconforming product before they occur. These actions contribute to continual quality improvement.

## What is it?

A constant search for ways to improve the QMS. Investigation and elimination of causes of non-conforming product, at any point in the process, distribution, and installation. Also, it is the procedures in use to prevent occurrence of nonconforming product in the first place.

 **How do I do it?**

- Continually improve (8.5.1) the QMS by using:
  - Quality policy
  - Objectives
  - Audit results
  - Data analysis
  - Corrective action
  - Preventive action
  - Management review
  - Customer feedback
  - Supplier performance

- Carry out corrective action (see Problem-Solving/Process-Improvement Model)

  - Assign responsibility to an individual or team

  - Review the number and significance of complaints and returns. Evaluate their importance

- ➜ Prepare a flow chart of the present system (See Flowcharting a Process)
- ➜ Evaluate the effectiveness of present practice
- ➜ Use problem-solving techniques:
    - ▶ Pareto
    - ▶ Fishbone analysis
    - ▶ Histograms
- ➜ Provide resources:
    - ▶ Expertise
    - ▶ Records, instruction procedures
    - ▶ Defective product (for analysis)
- ➜ Revise/improve methods and procedures to:
    - ▶ Investigate the cause of nonconformities
    - ▶ Analyze all processes
    - ▶ Determine a final fix  (i.e., an action plan)
    - ▶ Initiate action to prevent recurrence
    - ▶ Apply new controls
- ➜ Make permanent changes
- ➜ Evaluate revised procedures

- ➜ Carry out preventive action. (See Problem-Solving/Process-Improvement Model)
    - ➜ Assign responsibility to an individual or team
    - ➜ Review existing preventive action activities
    - ➜ Prepare a flow chart of the present system, i.e., IDEF0, Value Stream Mapping, etc.

- ◆ Evaluate the effectiveness of present practice
- ◆ Identify appropriate sources of information:
  - ▶ Reports of purchased materials' quality
  - ▶ Processes
  - ▶ Waiver concessions
  - ▶ Audit results
  - ▶ Quality records
  - ▶ Service reports
  - ▶ Customer complaints
- ◆ Identify activities in which preventive action activities can be established or enhanced
  *Examples*:
  - ▶ Product design
  - ▶ Process development
  - ▶ Process control
- ◆ Make use of preventive action tools such as Failure Mode and Effects Analysis (FMEA) see an example FMEA form on page 222
- ◆ Modify and continually improve controls to:
  - ▶ Identify potential nonconformities
  - ▶ Initiate action to prevent occurrence
  - ▶ Apply new controls
  - ▶ Report preventive actions that are taken
- ◆ Evaluate revised procedures
- ◆ Verify the effectiveness of the actions taken
- ◆ Submit actions for management review

## Examples of documents

- Customer complaint handling procedures
- Corrective action procedures (sub-clause 8.5.2)
- Preventive action procedures (sub-clause 8.5.3)

## Examples of records

- Record of nonconformance meriting assignment to the corrective action process
- Customer complaints
- Record of action taken on customer complaints
- Corrective action results (sub-clause 8.5.2)
- Preventive action results (sub-clause 8.5.3)

## Example of processes that might be applicable

- Continual improvement
- Corrective action
- Preventive action
- Root cause analysis
- Risk analysis
- Value stream analysis
- Lean enterprise initiatives

## Examples of linked processes

- Internal audit
- Analysis of data
- Management review
- Internal communication
- Continual improvement

##  Pitfalls

- A corrective action plan exists on paper, but is not being followed
- No person has been assigned responsibility for corrective/preventive action
- No formal preventive action plan exists, especially one that addresses product and process development in particular
- There is an emphasis on "troubleshooting" rather than prevention and continual improvement
- Inadequate capability to prevent recurrence of product failures

Example PFMEA form: see the AIAG FMEA reference manual, 4th Edition. For more information, visit www.aiag.org

**Potential Failure Mode and Effects Analysis (Process FMEA)**

FMEA Number _____

Page _____ of _____

Prepared by _____

FMEA Date (Orig.) _____

Item _____ Process Responsibility _____

Model Year(s)/Program(s) _____ Key Date _____

Core Team _____

| Process Step / Requirement / Function | Potential Failure Mode | Potential Effects of Failure | Severity | Classification | Potential Failure Mode | Controls Prevention | Current Process | | | Action Results | | | |
|---|---|---|---|---|---|---|---|---|---|---|---|---|---|
| | | | | | | | Occurrence | Controls Detection | RPN | Recommended Res. & Target Date | Severity | Occurrence Detection | RPN |

| Sub-Process Step | Failure Mode: First Evaluate failure mode before determining potential causes | Potential Causes | Scoring | | | | Decision Tree Analysis | | | | Action Type | | | Actions or Rationale for Stopping | Control Measures Currently Present | Outcome Measure(s) |
|---|---|---|---|---|---|---|---|---|---|---|---|---|---|---|---|---|
| | | | Severity | Probability | Hazard Score | Single point weakness? | Existing control measure? | Detectability | Proceed | A: Accept C: Control E: Eliminate | | | | | | |
| PRESCRIBING/ORDERING OF MEDICATIONS (1) | | | | | | | | | | | | | | | | |
| 1(a) Verbal or written order for critical meds | 1a(1) Physician orders are unclear (verbal orders) | Verbal orders not "repeated" back to physician; physician orders taken by a third party | 2 | 4 | 8 | Y | Y | N | | C | | | Implement dual review of orders by both pharmacy and nursing - faxing of orders to external pharmacy for pharmacy review, adding 24hr pharmacist | Verbal orders policy; transcription of physician orders policy; P&T rev/edu. trending of problematic prescribers | Monthly medical record review - review compliance; analysis of problematic prescribers |
| | 1a(2) Verbal orders not transcribed | Too busy to transcribe | 3 | 2 | 6 | Y | Y | N | | C | | | | Transcription of physician orders policy | |
| | 1a(3) Orders are not communicated to other staff members | Change of shift - orders not conveyed to incoming staff | 1 | 1 | 1 | N | Y | Y | | C | | | | Medication admin policy, sign off of phys. order form at change of shift | |
| | 1a(4) Illegible order | Transcribed incorrectly; can't read; poor handwriting | 3 | 4 | 12 | Y | Y | N | | E | | | P&T review; CPOE w/computer Phys Order Entry w/decision support | Transcription of physician orders policy; supervisor review of orders | |
| | 1a(5) Order entry not available | No pharmacist available; downtime | 2 | 3 | 6 | N | N | Y | | A | | | P&T review CPOE w/decision support | | |
| | 1a(6) Incorrect order | Conditions unknown to physician; medical record not available; record incomplete; physician unfamiliar with medication; duplication of therapy | 2 | 3 | 6 | N | Z | Y | | E | | | P&T review, physician education; CPOE w/decision support | | |

Preventative and Corrective Action Model

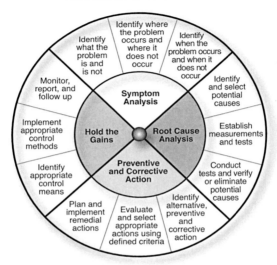

Information provided courtesy of
Ross Gilbert, GE Medical Systems

# NINE

# ISO 9001:2008 & CONTINUAL IMPROVEMENT EFFORTS

Continually improving after achieving
initial implementation ........................................ 226

Using ISO 9001:2008 for continual
improvement .......................................................... 227

Malcolm Baldrige National Quality Award ...... 230

MBNQA criteria ................................................... 232

ISO 9001:2008 and MBNQA ............................. 235

Other quality approaches ................................. 235

Tools and techniques resources ...................... 236

Environmental Management ............................. 239

## Continually improving after achieving initial implementation

ISO 9001:2008 requires that you have in place a business management system which assures your customers that your organization is capable of providing quality products and/or services. The Standards, basically, require that you identify your processes and then follow them as stated. This standard does not, however, ensure that the products and/or services produced from your processes are of quality by meeting all customer requirements.

The Standards, however, do form a necessary foundation for achieving quality products and services that will satisfy customers. The Standards are key to:

- Understanding your processes
- Communication of your process through appropriate methods
- Establishing controls of the processes
- Providing discipline to adhere to your processes

Securing implementation of a QMS, which likely would include registration, should be considered a milestone toward a comprehensive QMS. Soon after completing implementation of the process approach, your organization should consider the various options for improvement. They include using:

- ISO 9001:2008 for continual improvement
- ISO 9004, QMS guidelines
- ISO 19011:2002, guidelines for Quality Management System Auditing

- ➤ Malcolm Baldrige National Quality Award criteria

- ➤ Other quality approaches

The first step is to assess your organization's existing capabilities, using one or more of these approaches. Then, just as with the original planning for ISO 9001 registration, a plan for adopting a continual improvement system should be developed and followed.

### Using ISO 9001:2008 for Continual Improvement

The Standard has specific requirements for continual improvement built into it. The frequently used phrase "Say what you do, do what you say" is often used to describe compliance to a set of QMS standards. The phrase falls short of the intent of the Standard, however, because it implies that it is only necessary to adhere to established procedures.

ISO 9001:2008 contains requirements that are linked in a cycle of continual improvement:

> General Requirements (sub-clause 4.1)
>
> Quality Objectives (sub-clause 5.4.1)
>
> Management Review (sub-clause 5.6)
>
> Internal Audit (sub-clause 8.2.2)
>
> Improvement (sub-clause 8.5)

Some industries consider the following six themes from ISO 9001 as foundational to their supplemental improvement initiatives:

- Objectives for quality, and ensuring the effectiveness of the quality system
- Continual improvement
- Balance between documentation, skills, and training
- Design control
- Monitoring and measuring
- Customer satisfaction

To use ISO 9001:2008 effectively as a continual improvement methodology, follow the Plan-Do-Check-Act Cycle (see page 45).

- **PLAN** your objectives for quality, along with the processes to achieve them
- **DO** the appropriate resource allocation, implementation, training, and documentation
- **CHECK** to see if:
  - You are implementing as planned
  - Your quality system is effective and efficient
  - You are meeting your objectives for quality (product and process performance)
- **ACT** to improve the system as needed

Thus, ISO 9001:2008 is seen as a methodology for growth and improvement in capability. You should make use of the processes you might already have in place. These include:

**Setting objectives for quality.** These include both product and system improvements related to operating efficiencies and ultimately to cost control (see "clause 5, Management Responsibility," page 117).

**Internal Quality Audit.** Perform periodic auditing to verify that all systems are in place and continue to be effective, so opportunities for systems improvements can be noted and action taken (see "sub-clause 8.2.2, Internal Audit," page 194).

## Management review

▪ Ongoing review of progress in meeting:

  ▪ Operational objectives

  ▪ Overall business management system goals

▪ Periodic review (typically a quarterly review) of:

  ▪ Comprehensive system status

  ▪ Effectiveness of internal auditing

  ▪ Overall trends

  ▪ Results

  ▪ Goal setting for following year (See "sub-clause 5.6, Management Review," page 113)

**Corrective Action.** Identify nonconformances, both internal and external, as signals of opportunities for improvement, making process and product changes to prevent recurrence (see "sub-clause 8.5.2, Corrective Action," page 217).

**Preventive Action.** Identify potential problems before they occur by identifying deviations in patterns or trends in product or process performance. These trends may point to opportunities for improvement in product or process design (see "sub-clause 8.5.3, Preventive Action," page 218).

Information adapted from a paper by Donald Marquardt

# ⟨⟩ Malcolm Baldrige National Quality Award

Each year since 1988, a set of criteria has been published as a foundation for the examination process for America's Malcolm Baldrige National Quality Award (MBNQA), for which organizations may apply. Special criteria have recently been developed to allow organizations in education and health care sectors to also apply for the award.

The most visible part of the award program is the process of evaluating and selecting outstanding organizations that meet the stringent criteria of the award. Awards are presented each year by the President of the United States. Winners publicly describe the actions they took to become outstanding in their field. Similar award programs are in use in a large number of states, Europe, and many nations around the world.

The current MBNQA categories are listed on page 232. Many organizations are using the criteria of the MBNQA to judge their own current capabilities (self-assessment) and to set goals for improvements in quality. Criteria are updated each year; hence, they express state-of-the-art developments in quality management practice. The booklet describing the criteria is available at no cost from the National Institute of Standards and Technology office.

Contact:

**Malcolm Baldrige National Quality Award**
*National Institute of Standards and Technology*
Route 270 and Quince Orchard Road
Administration Building, Room A537
Gaithersburg, MD 20899-0001

Phone: (301) 975-2036
Email: nqp@nist.gov
www.quality.nist.gov

Bulk quantities are available at low cost from ASQ. Case studies developed for examiner training, and videos describing winners, are also available. See www.asq.org for more information.

# MBNQA Criteria

## 1.0 Leadership
    1.1   Organizational Leadership
    1.2   Social Responsibility

## 2.0 Strategic Planning
    2.1   Strategy Development
    2.2   Strategy Deployment

## 3.0 Customer and Market Focus
    3.1   Customer and Market Knowledge
    3.2   Customer Relationships and Satisfaction

## 4.0 Measurement, Analysis, and Knowledge Management
    4.1   Measurement and Analysis of Organizational Performance
    4.2   Information and Knowledge Management

## 5.0 Human Resource Focus
    5.1   Work Systems
    5.2   Employee Learning and Motivation
    5.3   Employee Well-being and Satisfaction

## 6.0 Process Management

6.1 Value Creation Processes

6.2 Support Processes

## 7.0 Business Results

7.1 Customer-focused Results

7.2 Product and Service Results

7.3 Financial and Market Results

7.4 Human Resource Results

7.5 Organizational Effectiveness Results

7.6 Governance and Social Responsibility Results

**How do ISO 9000 requirements align with Malcolm Baldrige National Quality Award (MBNQA) Criteria?**

● Very well aligned   ◐ Somewhat aligned   ○ Not aligned

| ISO 9001:2000 Quality System Standard | Leadership | Strategic Planning | Customer Focus | Information Analysis | Human Resources | Process Management | Business Results |
|---|---|---|---|---|---|---|---|
| 4 Quality Management System | ● | | ○ | ○ | | ● | ○ |
| 5.1 Management Commitment | ● | ○ | ● | ○ | | ● | ○ |
| 5.2 Customer Focus | ○ | ○ | ● | ○ | | ○ | ○ |
| 5.3 Quality Policy | ○ | ● | ○ | ○ | | ○ | ○ |
| 5.4 Planning | | ● | | ○ | | ○ | ● |
| 5.5 Resp., Authority and Commun. | | | ● | ● | | ● | ● |
| 5.6 Management Review | | ● | ○ | ● | | ○ | ○ |
| 6.1 Provision of Resources | ● | | | ○ | ○ | ○ | ● |
| 6.2 Human Resources | ● | ○ | ○ | ○ | ● | ● | ○ |
| 7.1 Planning of Product Realization | | ● | ○ | ○ | | ○ | ● |
| 7.2 Customer-related Processes | | | ● | ● | | ○ | ● |
| 7.3 Design and Development | | | ● | ● | | ○ | ● |
| 7.4 Purchasing | | | | ○ | | ● | ● |
| 7.5 Production/Service Provision | | ● | | ○ | | ● | ● |
| 7.6 Control/Monitoring/Meas. Devices | | | | ○ | | ○ | ● |
| 8.1 General | | | | ○ | | ● | ● |
| 8.2.1 Customer Satisfaction | ○ | ○ | ● | ● | ○ | ○ | ● |
| 8.2.2 Internal Audit | ● | ● | ○ | ● | ○ | ● | ○ |
| 8.2.3 Monitoring/Measurement Process | | ● | ○ | ● | | ● | ● |
| 8.2.4 Monitoring/Measurement Product | | ○ | ○ | ● | | ● | ○ |
| 8.3 Nonconforming Product | | | ● | ○ | | ● | ● |
| 8.4 Analysis of Data | ○ | ○ | ● | ● | ○ | ● | ● |
| 8.5 Improvement | ○ | | | ● | | ● | ○ |
| 8.5.2/3 Corrective/Preventive Action | ○ | | ● | ● | | ● | ● |

Adapted from *The ISO 9000 Handbook*, McGraw-Hill,
p. 529 (Updated to the current MBNQA criteria).
Reproduced with permission of The McGraw-Hill Companies.

# ISO 9001:2008 versus MBNQA

**↦** ISO 9001:2008 is more specific in the procedural items that are covered

**↦** ISO 9001:2008 makes some reference to most categories in the Baldrige Award criteria, including leadership, strategic planning, information and analysis, human resource focus, and process management

**↦** ISO 9001:2008 outlines an approach that most of the world-class organizations can be expected to follow in practice

**↦** The Baldrige Award criteria represent world-class performance

### Other quality approaches

Many organizations choose to adopt a philosophical approach to achieving quality improvement. Following the teachings of one or more of the quality and lean enterprise gurus (Dr. W. Edwards Deming, Dr. Joseph M. Juran, Philip B. Crosby, Dr. Kaoru Ishikawa, Dr. James P. Womack, etc.), these broadly based philosophies do not include specific requirements. Instead they advocate change in the organization's philosophy on quality, waste and variation reduction, management commitment, and organizational culture. These organizations work to create a structured system for creating organization-wide participation in planning and implementing a continual improvement process to meet and exceed customer needs. The basic principles include:

---

- ❧ Focusing on your customers and their needs

- ❧ Using data and data analysis to make decisions that continually improve the processes that produce quality products and services

- ❧ Involving everyone, both as individuals and team members, in the improvement efforts

- ❧ Using systems thinking and integrated planning

## Tools & Techniques Resource List

The following list of tools and techniques resources is a partial list to suggest further research:

Benchmarking:

> *The Search for Industry Best Practices that Lead to Superior Performance*, Robert Camp, Quality Press, Milwaukee, WI, 1989.

> *Benchmarking*, GOAL/QPC Research Committee Report, Salem, NH, 1991.

*Coach's Guide to The Memory Jogger™ II: The Easy-to-Use, Complete Reference for Working with Improvement and Planning Tools in Teams*, Michael Brassard, Diane Ritter, and others, GOAL/QPC, Salem, NH, 1995.

*Fundamental Concepts in the Design of Experiments*, Charles Hicks, Holt, Rinehart and Winston, New York, 1982.

*Fundamental Statistical Process Control Reference Manual*, Ford, Chrysler, General Motors, Southfield, MI, 1992.

Juran's Quality Control Handbook, 5th ed., J. M. Juran & F. Gryna, eds., McGraw-Hill Publishing Co., New York, 1999.

Quality Control and Industrial Statistics, Acheson J. Duncan, Irwin Professional Publishing, Homewood, IL, 1986.

SPC Simplified: Practical Steps to Quality, D. M. Amsden, R. T. Amsden, & H. Butler, Quality Resources, White Plains, NY, 1989.

Statistical Quality Control, 7th ed., E. L. Grant & R. Leavenworth, McGraw-Hill, New York, 1996.

The Goal: A Process of Ongoing Improvement, E. Goldratt & J. Cox, North River Press, Inc., Croton-on-Hudson, NY, 1992.

Lean Thinking: Banish Waste and Create Wealth In Your Corporation, Dr. James P. Womack and Daniel T. Jones, Free Press (A division of Simon & Schuster, Inc.), 1230 Avenue of the Americas, New York, NY., 1996 and 2003.

The Memory Jogger™ II, Michael Brassard & Diane Ritter, GOAL/QPC, Salem, NH, 1994.

The Memory Jogger Plus+®, Michael Brassard, GOAL/QPC, Salem, NH, 1989.

The Memory Jogger™ TS 16949:2002, James W. Collins Jr., GOAL/QPC, Salem, NH, 2005.

*Understanding Industrial Experimentation*, Donald Wheeler, SPC Press, Knoxville, TN, 1988.

*Understanding Statistical Process Control*, 2nd ed., D. Chambers & D. Wheeler, SPC Press, Knoxville, TN, 1992.

*Handbook of Statistical Methods for Engineers and Scientists*, Harrison Wadsworth, ed., McGraw-Hill, New York, 1990.

*Evolutionary Operation: A Statistical Method for Process Improvement*, G. Box & N. Draper, John Wiley & Sons, New York, 1969.

*Guide to Quality Control*, Kaoru Ishikawa, Asian Productivity Organization, Tokyo, 1982.

*The Lean Enterprise Memory Jogger*™, GOAL/QPC, Salem, NH, 2002.

*The Problem Solving Memory Jogger*™, GOAL/QPC, Salem, NH, 2000.

*The Process Management Memory Jogger*™, GOAL/QPC, Salem, NH, 2009.

*The Quality Audit Handbook*, J.P. Russell, Quality Press, Milwaukee, WI, 2000.

*After the Quality Audit*, J.P. Russell, Quality Press, Milwaukee, WI, 2000.

# ⟨⟩ Environmental Management

The success of ISO 9000 worldwide as a practical way for manufacturers to demonstrate that they meet an internationally recognized quality systems standards has established the feasibility of a similar coordination effort in environmental management (see page 5).

Following the process used in developing the ISO 9000 series, a family of environmental management standards has been developed by ISO/TC 207, with strong input from the United States and Canada. The structure and content of the work parallels ISO 9000 in many ways, including harmonizing auditor training criteria, and course provider and registrar accreditation processes as part of a coordinated QMS.

The United States has established an organizational liaison of the quality and environmental working groups developing and administering management systems standards in order to minimize duplication of effort. A list of the ISO/TC 207 standards issued as of this printing follows.

As with ISO 9000, environmental management standards do not dictate the actual performance standards to be met, such as for air and water quality, but coordinate processes and procedures for verifying that systems exist for controlling national environmental performance standards.

# Environmental Management Standards Issued

| ISO 14001 | Specification with guidance for use |
| ISO 14004 | Guidelines on principles, systems, and supporting techniques |
| ISO 14010 | Principles on environmental auditing |
| ISO 14011 | Audit procedures |
| ISO 14012 | Qualification criteria for environmental auditors |
| ISO 14015 | Environmental assessment of sites and entities |
| ISO 14020 | Goals and principles of all environmental labeling |
| ISO 14021–23 | Self-declaration environmental claims—terms and definitions |
| ISO 14024 | Environmental labels and declarations |
| ISO 14031 | Environmental performance evaluation |
| ISO 14040 | Life-cycle assessment |
| ISO 14041 | Life-cycle assessment—goal, scope, and inventory analysis |
| ISO 14042 | Life-cycle assessment—impact assessment |
| ISO 14043 | Life-cycle assessment—interpretation |
| ISO 14050 | Terms and definitions |
| ISO Guide 64 | Guide for the inclusion of environmental aspects in product standards |

# ISO/TC 207 on Environmental Management Organization Structure

| WG 1 | Environmental Aspects in Product Standards (Germany) |
| SC 1 | Environmental Management Systems (Great Britain) |
| SC 2 | Environmental Auditing and Related Environmental Investigations (Netherlands) |
| SC 3 | Environmental Labeling (Australia) |
| SC 4 | Environmental Performance Evaluation (U.S.) |
| SC 5 | Life-cycle Assessment (France/Germany) |
| SC 6 | Terms and Definitions (Norway) |

SC = Subcommittee
WG = Working group

# Chapter

# TEN

## ADDITIONAL RESOURCES

The ISO 9000 Standards Resources.............. 242

Supplements to ISO/TS 16949 ..................... 243

History of ISO 9000.................................... 246

ISO QMS Standards..................................... 247

Definitions of Key Terms and Acronyms ........ 249

References................................................. 253

# ◯ The ISO 9000 Standards Resources

The international standards issued are available through the national standards body in each country.

*United States:*
## American National Standards Institute
1819 L Street, NW, Sixth Floor
Washington, DC 20036
**Phone:** (202) 293-8020 | **Fax:** (202) 293-9287
www.ansi.org

*Canada:*
## CSA International
178 Rexdale Boulevard
Toronto, Ontario
Canada M9W 1R3
**Phone:** (416) 747-4000 | **Fax:** (416) 747-4149
www.csa-international.org

Many countries reissue and publish international standards as national standards under a separate designation. U.S. standards are available from:

### ASQ Quality Press
Customer Service Department
611 East Wisconsin Avenue, P. O. Box 3005
Milwaukee, WI 53201-3005
**Phone:** (800) 248-1946 | **Fax:** (414) 272-1734
www.qualitypress.asq.org

*The headquarters for ISO is:*
### International Organization for Standardization
1, ch. de la Voie-creuse, Case postale 56
CH-1211 Genève 20
Switzerland
**Phone:** 41 22 749 01 11 | **Fax:** 41 22 733 34 30
www.iso.ch

# ◯ Supplements to ISO/TS 16949

### Automotive Core Tools

The introduction to ISO/TS 16949, section 0.5, states:

> This Technical Specification, coupled with applicable customer-specific requirements, defines the fundamental quality management systems requirements for those subscribing to this document.

Customer-specific requirements include the use of core tools that are expected, approved, and/or required by a particular customer. An organization must know and meet all customer requirements, including any required core tools.

Other subscribing customers might have other core-tool requirements than the ones listed here. An example is the German VDA 6.3.

### Current North American core tools include the following:

### Production Part Approval Process (PPAP)

If your customer requires this tool, then it is a requirements document, not a reference manual.

ISO/TS 16949 *clause reference*: 4.2.3.1; 4.2.4; 5.4.2; 7.1; 7.3.7; 7.5.1; 8.3

This document covers generic requirements for production part approval for all production and service commodities, including bulk materials. It applies whether these commodities are produced internally by the automotive manufacturers or externally by outside suppliers.

### Advanced Product Quality Planning (APQP) and Control Plan

ISO/TS 16949 *clause reference*: 5.5; 7.1; 7.5

This reference manual is to communicate to suppliers (both internal and external) and sub-contractors the common product-quality planning and control-plan guidelines developed jointly by Chrysler (now DaimlerChrysler), Ford, and General Motors. The manual provides guidelines designed to produce a product-quality plan that supports the development of a product or service that will satisfy the customer.

For some automotive customers, the terms *product realization* and *advanced product quality planning* are interchangeable.

### Potential Failure Mode and Effects Analysis (FMEA)

ISO/TS 16949 *clause reference*: 5.4.2; 7.1; 7.3

An FMEA can be described as a systemized group of activities intended to:

1. Recognize and evaluate the potential failure of a product or process and its effects.

2. Identify actions that could eliminate or reduce the chance of the potential failure occurring.

3. Document the process.

## Measurement Systems Analysis (MSA)

ISO/TS 16949 clause reference: 7.6.1

Because measurement plays such a significant role in helping a facility accomplish its mission, the quality of the systems that produce those measurements must be assessed. If the quality level is too low, the facility might not be able to accomplish the task at hand. For example, too much variation in a measurement system being used for statistical process control (SPC) could mask important variations in the manufacturing process, resulting in the facility's inability to exploit the competitive advantages of using SPC.

## Fundamental Statistical Process Control (SPC)

ISO/TS 16949 *clause reference*: 8.1.1; 8.1.2

In the past, the automotive industry had no unified formal approach to SPC. Certain manufacturers provided methods for their suppliers, while others had no specific requirements. In an effort to simplify and to minimize variation in supplier quality requirements, Chrysler, Ford, and General Motors agreed to develop and distribute this manual, which should be considered an introduction to SPC.

# History of ISO 9000

The International Organization for Standardization (ISO) was formed in 1946 in Geneva, Switzerland. The ISO's intention was to promote the development of international standards and related activities, to foster the increased trade of products and services between countries.

The ISO, made up of Technical Committees (TC), formed TC 176 specifically to address standardization issues relating to quality management and quality assurance. Subcommittees were established to determine common terminology, to develop quality systems standards, and to develop supplementary technical standards that were issued as additional standards in the ISO 9000 and ISO 10000 series.

The ISO 9000 standards have been mandated by many governments and organizations around the world. Countries continue to have input into the ongoing development and improvement of the Standards. According to ISO procedures, all ISO 9000 standards are reviewed and revised or reaffirmed once every five years.

TC 176 now has issued a number of additional quality management standards, guidelines, technical specifications, and technical reports in the ISO 9000 and ISO 10000 series. These are listed on the following pages.

# ISO QMS Standards and Other Publications

### Quality Management and Quality Assurance Standards

ISO 9000:2005     QMS—Fundamentals and vocabulary

ISO 9001:2008     QMS—Requirements

ISO 9004:2000     QMS—Guidelines for performance improvements (this is in revision at the time of this publication)

### Other International Standards

ISO 10005:2005     QMS—Guidelines for quality plans

ISO 10006-2003     QMS—Guidelines for quality plans

Supporting technologies (some are under development at the time this publication is being written)

ISO 10001:2007     Quality management—Customer satisfaction—Guidelines for codes of conduct for organizations

ISO 10002:2004     Quality management—Customer satisfaction—Guidelines for complaints handling in organizations

ISO 10003:2004     Quality management—Customer satisfaction

| | – Guidelines for dispute resolution external to organizations |
| --- | --- |
| ISO/CD TS 10004 | Quality management – Customer satisfaction – Guidelines for monitoring and measuring |
| ISO 10012:2003 | Measurement management systems – Requirements for measurement processes and measuring equipment |
| ISO 10013:2001 | Guidelines for QMS documentation |
| ISO 10014:2006 | Quality management – Guidelines for realizing financial and economic benefits |
| ISO 10015:1999 | Quality management – Guidelines for training |
| ISO 10017:2003 | Guidance on statistical techniques for ISO 9001:2000 |
| ISO/AWI 10018 | Quality management – Guidelines on people involvement and competencies |
| ISO 10019:2005 | Guidelines for the selection of QMS consultants and use of their services |
| ISO/WD 19011 | Guidelines for auditing management systems |
| ISO 19011:2002 | Guidelines for quality and/or environmental management systems auditing |

# Definitions of Key Terms and Acronyms

Definitions identified with a clause number are taken from ANSI/ISO/ASQ Q9000 *(reprinted with permission of the American Society for Quality)*.

**Accreditation** is the formal recognition that a registration organization is competent to carry out the process of registration to the ISO 9000 standards/QS-9000 Requirements.

**ANSI** is the American National Standards Institute.

**ASQ** is the American Society for Quality.

**Certificate** is a written statement issued by an authorized body stating that an organization has complied with a set of standards or requirements.

**Compliance** is the affirmative indication or judgment that the supplier of a product or service has met the requirements of the relevant specifications, contract, or regulation.

**Conformance:** *See compliance.*

**Control chart** is a graphical method for evaluating whether a process is or is not in a "state of statistical control."

**CQI** is Continuous Quality Improvement.

**CSA International** is the Standards Association of Canada.

**Design review** is a formal, documented, comprehensive, and systematic examination of the status of a design to evaluate the design input requirements against the capability of the design to meet these input requirements, and to identify problems and propose solutions (clause 3.11).

---

**Documentation of the QMS** is a systematic and understandable description and transcription of those policies and procedures affecting product and service quality.

**EOQ** is the European Organization for Quality.

**EU** is the European Union.

**Inspection** is the conformity evaluation by observation and judgment accompanied by measurement, testing, or gauging (clause 3.8.2).

**ISO** is the International Organization for Standardization.

**Management review** is the review of the quality system by management to ensure the quality system remains suitable and effective.

**MBNQA** is the Malcolm Baldrige National Quality Award.

**Organization** is a group of people and facilities with an orderly arrangement of responsibilities, authorities, and relationships.

**$P_{pk}$** is the performance index, typically defined as the minimum of $\dfrac{USL - \bar{\bar{X}}}{3\hat{\sigma}_s}$ or $\dfrac{\bar{\bar{X}} - LSL}{3\hat{\sigma}_s}$

**Procedures** are the documented practice(s) defining the who, what, and when of quality activities. Procedures are typically used at the departmental level, and may involve more than one department.

**Process capability** is the total range of inherent variation in a stable process.

**Process control** is the identification of, and action, on all identified factors affecting process variability, including materials accepted into the process, proper maintenance of equipment, use of statistical process control methods, and degree of adherence to valid work instructions.

**Quality** is the degree to which a set of inherent characteristics fulfills requirements (clause 3.1.1).

**Quality assurance** is the part of quality management that is focused on providing confidence that quality requirements will be fulfilled.

**Quality audit** is the systematic, independent, and documented process for obtaining audit evidence and evaluating it objectively to determine the extent to which agreed criteria are fulfilled (clause 3.9.1).

**Quality control** is the part of quality management focused on fulfilling quality requirements.

**Quality management** is the coordinated activities to direct and control an organization with regard to quality.

**Quality Management System** is a set of inter-related or interacting processes with regard to quality, accomplished by the management of an organization by establishing policy and objectives, and by achieving those objectives (clause 3.2.1,-2,-3).

**Quality manual** is the document specifying the quality management system of an organization (clause 3.7.4).

**Quality planning** is the part of quality management focused on setting quality objectives and specifying necessary operational processes and related resources to fulfill the quality objectives (clause 3.2.9).

**Quality policy** is the overall intentions and direction of an organization related to quality as formally expressed by top management (clause 3.2.4).

**Registrar** is the company that conducts quality system assessment to a recognized quality systems standard or set of requirements.

**Registrar Accreditation Board** is an affiliate of the ASQ that recognizes the competence and reliability of

---

registrars of quality systems, and works to achieve international recognition of registrations issued by accredited registrars.

**Registration** is the procedure by which an organization indicates that it fulfills the requirements for a QMS and then is included or registered in an appropriate public list.

**Specification** is the document that prescribes the requirements that the product or service has to meet.

**Statistical process control** is the application of statistical techniques to the control of processes.

**Statistical quality control** is the application of statistical techniques to the control of product quality.

**Supplier** is an organization or person that provides a product.

**Testing** is a means of determining the capability of an item to meet specified requirements by subjecting the item to a set of physical, chemical, environmental, or operating actions and conditions.

**Traceability** is the ability to trace the history, application, or location of that which is under consideration (clause 3.5.4).

**TQM** is Total Quality Management.

## References

- *Coach's Guide to The Memory Jogger™ II*, Michael Brassard, Diane Ritter, and others, GOAL/QPC, Salem, NH, 1995.

- *Coach's Guide* Training Package. Includes the Coach's Guide, 5 copies of The Memory Jogger™ II, and 187 overheads on CD-ROM, GOAL/QPC, Salem, NH, 1996.

- *The Lean Enterprise Memory Jogger™*, GOAL/QPC, Salem, NH, 2002.

- *The Memory Jogger™ II*, Michael Brassard & Diane Ritter, GOAL/QPC, Salem, NH, 1994.

- *The Memory Jogger Plus+®*, Michael Brassard, GOAL/QPC, Salem, NH, 1989.

- *The Memory Jogger™ TS 16949:2002*, James W. Collins Jr., GOAL/QPC, Salem, NH, 2005.

- *The Problem Solving Memory Jogger™*, GOAL/QPC, Salem, NH, 2000.

- *The Process Management Memory Jogger™*, GOAL/QPC, Salem, NH, 2009.

- *The Team Memory Jogger™*, GOAL/QPC (Salem, NH) and Oriel (Madison, WI), 1995.

For a listing of more specialized reference books, see page 236 and page 247.

# ⊕ Index

## A

Advanced Product Quality Planning (APQP) and Control Plan, 244

American National Standards Institute (ANSI), 2, 242, 249

American Society for Quality (ASQ), 231, 249

analysis of data, 212–216

ASQ Quality Press, 242

auditing
first-party, 3
internal, 78
preparation checklist, 78
preparation for, 72–74
for registration, 78–80
second-party, 3
steps involved, 34–36
surveillance, 80–82
third-party, 78

auditors, working with, 75–76

automotive core tools, 243

## C

Canadian Standards Association (CSA), 242, 249

capability indices, 67

certification, defined, 8

certification, vs. registration, 8

Certification Bodies (CBs), 74

common cause, 65

consultants
role of, 76–77
working with, 77

continual improvement, 12–13, 217
after achieving initial implementation, 226–227
environmental management, 239–240
ISO 9001:2008 and, 227–229

Malcolm Baldrige National Quality Award (MBNQA), 230–231

tools and techniques resource list, 236–238

**continuous quality improvement** (CQI), 249

**contract review process**, 142–143

suggested process steps, 142

what to consider in contract, 142–143

**control charts**, 65–66

**core process mapping**, 31

**customer focus**, 9

**customer oriented processes** (COPs), 20

**customer property**, 172–175

**customer-related processes**, 138–142

# D

**data analysis**, 212–216

**decision making**

determining appropriate amount of documentation, 42

factual approach to, 13

gap analysis, 42

over-documentation, 42

questions driving in process based organization, 37–41

**design and development**, 143–151

**documents, defined**, 46

# E

**environmental management**, 239–240

**Environmental Management Systems** (EMS), 5–7

# F

**factual approach to decision making**, 13

**flowcharting**, 61–64

**Fundamental Statistical Process Control** (SPC), 245

## G

gap analysis, 42

## I

identification and traceability, 167–171

improvement, 216–224

internal audits, 194–199

International Organization for Standardization (ISO), defined, 2

involvement of people, quality management principles and, 10–11

ISO 9000

  core standards, 4–5

  defined, 2

  history of, 246

  reasons for adopting, 7–8

  requirements, 9–14

ISO 9001:2008

  continual improvement and, 227–229

  internal and external customer satisfaction, 43–44

  lessons learned in implementing, 84

  management responsibility, 87–88

  measurement, analysis, and improvement, 91–92

  product realization, 89–91

  QMS requirements, 86, 86–87

  resource management, 88–89

  summary of content, 85

ISO/TS 16949 users, ix

## L

leadership, quality managment principles and, 10

## M

Malcolm Baldrige National Quality Award (MBNQA), 230–231, 235, 250

  criteria, 232–234

  ISO 9001:2008 vs., 235–236

management representatives, 119

management responsibility

applicable processes, 116

explained, 110

guidance in preparing documents, 115

guidance in preparing quality policy, 114

implementing, 110–114

ISO 9001:2008, 87–88

management representatives, 119

management review, 119

measurables, 116–117

pitfalls, 117–118

quality policy, 118

why to use, 109

Measurement Systems Analysis (MSA), 245

monitoring and measuring

equipment, 181–186

overview, 190–193

processes, 199–202

products, 203–208

mutually beneficial supplier relationships, 13–14

## N

nonconforming product, control of, 208–211

## O

octopus model, 30

over-documentation, 42

## P

Plan–Do–Check–Act (PDCA) Cycle, 45, 59

planning realization, 133–138

Potential Failure Mode and Effects Analysis (FMEA), 244

problem-solving/process improvement model, 59–60

**process approach**

collecting, organizing, and reporting data and information, 67–68

control charts, 65–66

core process mapping, 31

customer oriented processes (COPs) examples, 20

documents vs. records, 46

explained, 11

flowcharting, 61–64

implementing to QMS, 34–37

improving work processes, 58–59

ISO 9001:2008, 43–44

octopus model, 30

overview, 16–17

Plan-Do-Check-Act (PDCA) Cycle, 45

preparing other documentation, 56–57

preparing work/job instructions, 54–55

problem-solving/ process improvement model, 59–60

process capability, 66–67

process control system, 64–65

process models, 29–30

Quality Manual, 47–48

quality procedures, 49–53

support and management processes, 21–27

Terrapene, 27

value of, 18–19

value stream mapping, 32–33

**process capability,** 66–67

**process control system,** 64–65

**process models,** 29–30

defined, 29

why to use, 29–30

**processes, validation of,** 163–167

**product realization, ISO**

9001:2008, 89–91

production and service provisions, 158–163

Production Art Approval Process (PPAP), 243

products, preservation of, 176–180

purchasing, 151–157

# Q

quality management principles, 9–14

    continual improvement, 12–13

    customer focus, 9

    factual approach to decision making, 13

    involvement of people, 10–11

    leadership, 10

    mutually beneficial supplier relationships, 13–14

    process approach, 11

    system approach, 11–12

Quality Management System (QMS)

    control of documents, 98–99

    defined, 3

    explained, 96

    implementing, 96–97

    implementing process approach to, 34–37

    measurables, 97–98

    pitfalls, 102–103

    preparing quality manual, 98

    records control, 99

    requirements for ISO 9001:2008, 86–87

    why to use, 95

Quality Manual, 47–48

quality procedures, 49–53

# R

records, defined, 46

registrars

    role of, 74

    selecting, 74–75

    working with, 75–76

resource management

    explained, 123–124

implementing,
124–125

ISO 9001:2008,
88–89

measurables, 127–128

pitfalls, 128

why to use, 123

# S

statistical methods,
202–203

support and manage-
ment processes,
21–27

input, 22–23

main processes, 22

output, 23

process identification,
24

subprocesses, 22

turtles, 25–26

system approach, 11–12

# T

Terrapene, 27

# V

validation, 151

value stream mapping,
32–33

verification, 151

# W

work processes, im-
proving, 58–59

work/job instructions,
54–55